MODERN
etiquette
MADE EASY

M⬤DERN
etiquette
MADE EASY

*A Five-Step Method
to Mastering Etiquette*

Myka Meier

Skyhorse Publishing

Skyhorse Publishing books may be purchased in bulk at special discounts
for sales promotion, corporate gifts, fund-raising, or educational purposes.
Special editions can also be created to specifications. For details, contact
the Special Sales Department, Skyhorse Publishing, 307 West 36th Street,
11th Floor, New York, NY 10018 or info@skyhorsepublishing.com.

Skyhorse® and Skyhorse Publishing® are registered trademarks of Skyhorse
Publishing, Inc.®, a Delaware corporation.

Visit our website at www.skyhorsepublishing.com.

10 9 8

Library of Congress Cataloging-in-Publication Data is available on file.

Cover design by Daniel Brount
Cover images by You Look Lovely Photography, Brook Christopher,
and gettyimages

Print ISBN: 978-1-5107-4777-7
Ebook ISBN: 978-1-5107-4778-4

Printed in China

Lovingly dedicated to my kind, strong (and polite!),
beautiful little Valentina

Contents

Introduction

Don't Fake It Until You Make It—Practice It Until You Become It

Hello, hello! I'm so glad you're here. If you're reading this, perhaps you've decided you're ready for a change. Maybe you want to completely revamp yourself, or maybe you just want a bit of social polishing. Perhaps you grew up in a formal environment and want to brush up, or maybe you grew up with not much at all and look forward to learning A to Z. Regardless of your background, you should be excited, because soon after reading this book, people will start to comment on how you seem "different . . . in a good way, of course!" Why? Because you will appear a bit more elegant, a splash more sophisticated, extra confident, and more charismatic. Soon you'll realize that not only do you feel more polished, but you'll also notice you're turning more heads. You will, after all, be practicing the Five-Step Meier Method, taught throughout this book to give you an upper edge in all areas of your life. What you'll learn in the following chapters isn't rocket science, but promises to offer practical, modern, and relatable tips that you can start using instantly.

This book is broken down into the five easy steps needed to completely transform yourself through, you guessed it, etiquette. Through the Five-Step Meier Method, you will learn how to first *transform* yourself, then how to *attract* the type of people and life you want, how to feel *empowered* and exude confidence, how to *thrive* socially, and finally, how to *practice* it daily.

The Five-Step Meier Method

1. TRANSFORM
2. ATTRACT
3. EMPOWER
4. THRIVE
5. PRACTICE

Easy, right? Don't worry, I will be guiding you through every step of the process. You see, long ago I realized that etiquette is an avenue to confidence and success, and I created the Meier Method to help other people realize that, too.

Now, first things first. Etiquette is much more than you maybe even knew. When people come to me to learn, they often think they will walk away with a better understanding of how to hold a fork and knife and sit up straight. *Sigh.* This would be so dull. Etiquette, my friends, is *way* more than this! Etiquette is actually this fabulous way of conducting yourself to show respect, consideration, and kindness to those around you. It's putting everyone and all living things before yourself. It's about practicing social and emotional intelligence, or EQ (emotional quotient). The bonus is the polishing part. To put yourself together and look exquisite is not just about making yourself feel great, but about making the people around you feel special that you got all razzle dazzled up for them. See? In the end it's still all about showing others respect through your actions. It's an extra advantage that you look dashing in the end, too!

When people start noticing these subtle (and some not-so-subtle) differences, they'll want to know your secret. If or when you tell people you are reading an etiquette book, they will likely say one of the following statements, so let me just address them up front.

1. **"Etiquette is outdated, a lost art form . . . dare I say it, antiquated."**

Actually, etiquette is arguably more relevant today than ever before. With examples such as new forms of electronic communication, gender equality, and international travel, we have had to rewrite the rules of etiquette in many instances. We are so attached to our cell phones and devices that we forget how to communicate in person, how to eat around a table, or socialize without checking a phone. Society is evolving and changing so rapidly, that we must change with it.

2. **"Etiquette is stuffy and only for the 1 percent."**

Au contraire. Etiquette is for everyone and you don't have to have a penny to learn it or practice it. You can learn it online, in school, and even from your parents or grandparents. In all my years training and instructing etiquette, I bet you'll never guess where, to this day, after more than sixty-five countries and countless cities, I would award the best etiquette. The most jaw-dropping display of good etiquette I have ever witnessed was in a tiny village on the outskirts of a hippo bog in Zambia. The villagers didn't have two pennies to rub together, but I still get goosebumps thinking about how incredibly selfless and thoughtful these people were. I was sleeping in a canvas tent which had a lock on it, literally so no animal could enter in the night, and in the morning, I was instructed to blow my given whistle when I was ready to come out. Within what seemed like half a second later, a figure stood at my tent. As the doorway opened, there stood a man with the warmest smile, holding his hand out to help me. With a bit of a graceful bow at the waist, he helped me step over the ledge. As

I stepped out, I felt something over my head. I looked up, surprised to see an umbrella made out of animal hide hovering overhead. "Oh, you are so kind, but it's not raining!" With a smile, the man said, "It's to protect you from the dew drops." Shrugging my shoulders in return, I began to walk out of the tent toward the breakfast area. As I walked, I heard a *clop, clop, clop* sound and realized quarter-sized drops of water from the sausage trees above were landing on the hide umbrella being carried over my head. As I continued walking, I heard a rustling behind me. I turned to see another man rolling up a carpet that I had been walking on. The man saw that I noticed him and said, "Pardon me, ma'am. I simply laid this down earlier so that you would not sink into the mud as you walked outside of your tent." I couldn't believe my eyes. I wasn't anyone important, but in that moment, I felt like the most important person on earth. As I arrived at the breakfast table, the seat was pulled out and tucked in behind me. As I looked over the table, which had been beautifully set, I was startled to feel a shawl being delicately placed over my shoulders. "So that you don't feel cold, Madam," another man said. I wondered what he meant, as I was in Africa, but obliged anyway. As I sipped my coffee, a gust of wind breezed over the camp and the chill on my face reminded me that my shoulders were fully covered. These people had thought of everything! They literally knew what I needed before I even knew I needed it myself. This is the epitome of good etiquette, taking care of others and making them feel comfortable and respected, especially when in your care. Not a stuffy, pretentious bone in their bodies, and with nothing financially to show, yet they were the most gracious people on earth.

3. **"Etiquette is mostly about dining and you only use it when you go to 'fancy' places. Oh, and if you set a nice table with lots of pretty tableware, it's a bit pretentious or showy."**

Introduction

If you go to someone's home (or restaurant) and they have set a formal or "fancy" table with so much silver, china, and crystal that it's dizzying, some might think it's a bit too much. Too over the top, or ostentatious, if you will. What I like to point out here is that setting a table with all the pieces needed to enjoy the meal is excellent etiquette of the host. After all, the host took the time and effort to lay everything out and make sure it was sparkling and organized specially for you so that when you sat down you felt important. It's such a compliment when someone sets a gorgeous table for another. While dining is an important aspect of etiquette, eating in a well-mannered way is all about respect for others, simply so that everyone around you can enjoy their meal without being distracted. As we often dine while socializing, etiquette over meals and around a table remains an important aspect of social and business etiquette.

4. **"If you know all the rules, can set a table, and eat in a posh way, you must have good etiquette, right?"**

Some people think that if they are well-dressed, immaculately groomed, and perfectly poised, they must already have great etiquette. Now, if they have all of these things but walk into a room and don't act in a friendly manner, I would argue their etiquette is far from perfect. Imagine someone entering a cocktail party, dressed to perfection with a spectacular dress or head-turning blazer, and greet all their friends but ignore the others they have not met before. Maybe there is even someone standing in the near corner by themselves. A man or woman with exceptional etiquette would not only introduce themselves to everyone within the immediate area they had not yet met, but would also make a special trip over to the person who didn't know anyone and invite them to join the group. That would be way more impressive than the fabulous outfit any day.

I'd love for you to start thinking about etiquette in this way. This is, after all, the root of what etiquette is all about and what the Meier Method is based on, with all lessons going back to this very thought process. If you take nothing else away from this book, please take that. Okay, and maybe please also hold your cutlery correctly.

Now, when people take my etiquette courses, they often arrive and are a combination of intimidated, shy, excited, and terrified at the same time. They truly expect that I am going to be a formal, prissy, prudish woman hitting them on the knuckles with a ruler to sit up straight. This couldn't be further from the truth. I love to laugh and look at the humorous and positive side of everything, and my very favorite thing on the planet is seeing people leave my courses happier and more confident than when they walked in. In this book I'll be sharing everything you will need to know in order to look and feel phenomenal, have the confidence to navigate through a twelve-course meal, and be the social envy of any room. Thought you were just picking up an old etiquette book, eh?

I'll start by telling you the story of how I got to where I am today, so it may give you the encouragement to know that you can learn it, too. I always tell people that if I can do it, just about anyone can! What matters isn't your gender, background, or career, but more your willingness to make changes and to be excited to practice what you learn. Some people say "fake it until you make it," but I don't believe that theory. Instead, I'll leave you with two Myka-isms (My-kah-iz-im: An inspirational quote, acronym, listicle, or theory from Myka to help you feel fabulous). "Learn it and then you earn it," which really means "practice it until you become it."

Meier Method Step 1

TRANSFORM

Welcome to step 1 of The Five Step Meier Method! I consider this step important in laying a strong foundation for the transformation you are about to undergo. It's the step that is the most visual, where people will start noticing the "new you" and will give you an instant confidence boost. Not only will heads begin to turn, but you'll also be learning practical tips that you can start using instantly (yes, as in today!) to look and feel more confident and polished. Get excited to invest the much-deserved time into yourself . . . because a happier, more confident you will also benefit everyone around you. I warned you this isn't your grandmother's etiquette book!

©Brook Christopher

Chapter 1

My Transformation Story

Raised in a modest household, I'm not even sure I touched a real silver fork until the age of twenty. I grew up near the intersection of Cattleman and Beeridge Road (as in bumble bee) in Sarasota, Florida in a neighborhood where there were as many cows as kids. To say we were raised in a casual household may be an understatement, as I spent the majority of my childhood in flip-flops running around muddy orange groves. My sweet father, a Caribbean immigrant who arrived in the US via sailboat, and my loving and free-spirited mother from Boston, had decidedly raised us with all the wealth that only love could bring. While we didn't have much financially, my parents showered my two brothers and I with attention and affection. Although I may not have been taught what a fish fork looked like, I was taught to show respect to everyone around me from a very young age. I was the little girl who protected bugs from being squashed, stuck up for the little ones on the playground, and always called an adult by their surname.

Looking back, my upbringing was one of the greatest gifts I was ever given, as it taught me later in life to be grateful for everything and that I needed to work hard for what I wanted. There is a simple, wonderful thing about growing up without knowing brand names or overvaluing possessions.

In fact, my childhood could not have been farther from my current life in Manhattan. When I'm not in a grand ballroom teaching etiquette courses to groups of well-educated clients on how to walk down marble staircases in heels, tie a tie, eat oysters, twirl spaghetti, and how to be the most social person in a room, I'm probably sneaking to the back of The Plaza Hotel's kitchen with my heels kicked off, testing the chef's most recent batch of macaroons. I have been affectionately nicknamed by the white gloved doormen of the hotel as "grown-up Eloise," Eloise being a cheeky and mischievous fictional children's book character who lives in The Plaza Hotel. You see, while I know all the rules, I would be rather dull if I followed them all the time! The inner little girl covered in mud will always be there, only now I get to play in a shiny castle in Manhattan. I may look a bit more polished, but I'll never be serious, unapproachable, or practice anything but kindness (and if you look carefully, you may still be able to find some orange sap in my hair).

Rewind to the age of twenty-five, and I had just arrived on a work visa to London. I had always wanted to live abroad, but now that I was here, I was so overwhelmed. I remember arriving to dinner in elegant Sloane Square in my jeans and chunky-knitted sweater, and the feeling of wanting to crawl under the table and hide when I realized everyone around me was dressed in beautiful flowing fabrics, tailored jackets, and polished shoes. Underdressed and mortified, the first course of the meal came. I froze in panic when I realized I had no idea which fork or knife to use from the six or so laid out, and what on earth was that tiny little spoon for? I carefully observed as everyone around me confidently laughed and chatted and didn't even seem to notice the complex jungle of china and crystal in front of them. So relaxed, so sophisticated, and so glamorous, but all without trying. They all ate in a way that looked almost synchronized, and how did everyone know to hold silverware that way? Apparently, there was an exact way to hold a wine glass, too. I thoroughly disliked this feeling of ignorance, and worst of all found that it left me feeling the least confident I have ever felt in my life, so I decided to fully immerse myself in my new culture and enroll in an etiquette course at the suggestion of my suave Swiss boyfriend Marco (what's worse is that he even felt the need to have to propose it).

Now, until this point, like many people, I thought etiquette was stuffy and only for the wealthy. This, I soon would learn, could not be further from the truth. I arrive for my first etiquette lesson at a gorgeous building in London that is hundreds of years old and has so many winding staircases, vaulted ceilings, and life-size oil paintings of lords and ladies that I wonder if it was at one time a royal residence. While I am twenty minutes early (which I later learn is impolite, as it may rush your host), Diana, my etiquette instructor, glides through the door exactly as the chime of the old grandfather clock dings. She is petite and pretty, somewhere likely in her fifties, wearing a striking blue dress and donning a neat blonde bob. She commands the room as she enters with the most wonderful energy and presence. All heads turn her way. She is the most charming and charismatic person I have met in as long as I can remember. She is magnetic and I am instantly intrigued.

Diana introduces herself over a cup of tea, all while walking me through how to properly drink it from a teacup. I tell her my short-version life story in twenty minutes, including my biggest insecurities of not fitting in, and instantly feel better, as though I am in a therapy session. In the most beautiful and clear British accent, she assures me I am in the best of hands and put me at immediate ease, which I also learn is the sign of a good host.

She explains to me that etiquette is all about being kind and considerate to everyone. It's about understanding a culture and those in it so that we can all live together respectfully. It's about putting others first. She explains that part of showing respect to others is to present ourselves in our best light, from making a first impression to being clearly able to communicate and converse. She gives the example of dressing neatly as being a polite way to show you have put effort into your appearance, and a sign of respect to yourself and others. Another example she gives is dining etiquette. We must know which fork and knife to dine with and how to hold them properly so we can focus on enjoying conversation with our dining companion and not be nervous about making a mistake. We also don't want to scare away a date, offend a potential business partner, or be rude to a social acquaintance by a mishap that could have easily been prevented. I quickly realize her job is to instill both knowledge and confidence in me.

How did I have this all so wrong in the first place? I wanted to learn etiquette because I thought it would just physically polish me, but what I learned that first day is that it is so much more than that. I am so enamored by this ideology of etiquette that I am like a horse with blinders on, focused on her every word. It all suddenly makes sense.

We talk about how etiquette is sadly seen as a lost art form that people deem less and less necessary. There is a tiny bit of sadness in her voice when she says this may be the last generation to care but she hopes that is not the case. I learned on that day that etiquette is all about compassion, kindness, and empathy for others. I suddenly see how these skills relate to my life in so many ways, and realize that it is essentially teaching people to hone in on their emotional intelligence.

Realizing she's now behind on timing, she asks me if I'm ready for some fun. She knows I'm one of her tribe and soaking up every glorious second. I feel like I am in the movie *The Princess Diaries,* and am in heaven. We spend the entire day together, laughing and practicing my new skills. We go over formal dining etiquette, cultural etiquette, and social graces. It's all so interesting that hours seem like minutes and soon I'm told my course is over. I am so inspired (and slightly embarrassed about how much I didn't know) that I leave feeling high on life. My day ends and I feel confident and empowered. I want to call all the girls back home and tell them everything I learned and share my newfound knowledge with anyone who will listen.

I am addicted to the way I feel when I walk into the store later that same day to buy what are called "biscuits" in London, which are really cookies in the US. I enroll in another finishing school, and another . . . and another. I learn to walk graciously and how to climb staircases with perfect posture (posture is a body language sign to others that you're attentive and alert). I can't stop myself. I am near obsessed with how much I have to learn and the way it makes me feel when I practice it. I spend near every penny I own on instruction from any and all schools I can find. I eventually begin training underneath Alexandra Messervy, a former member of staff of the Queen of England's household. I hear stories of Princess Diana at Balmoral and learn about the same type of training and techniques that would be taught within palace walls. Alexandra later on became a fabulous mentor to me. I leave my sessions floating on air. I suddenly feel as if I have taken on an alter ego—but I love it. I love the way people react to me and treat me, and I love the way I treat myself most of all.

I continue to absorb the culture and people I admire around me like a sponge. While now I truly understand the essence of what etiquette is, I do also rather enjoy the "polishing" part, too. Because I live in the same zip code as Kensington Palace, I get my nails done at the same place as Kate Middleton, the future Duchess of Cambridge, and my nail technician tells me the exact nail color she wears. Later that same week, I tell a journalist friend about this bit of firsthand knowledge and within twenty-four hours every website around the world writes about "Kate's nail color of choice." I start to feel more comfortable socializing in British circles and get invited to a few neighborhood parties and events where the royals are. I dance one night with Prince Harry at a club and see both Prince William and Prince Harry out at social events and restaurants. I'm wearing things I never thought I would have the confidence to try on, and find I am no longer fearful to walk up to anyone I find appealing to introduce myself. Before I know it, I have a phone full of new friends and invitations. While many partners would disapprove of my newfound social prowess, Marco beams with pride watching me blossom. I realize that everything I'm learning and practicing is allowing me to grow into the woman I always knew I could be, but I know I still have so much to learn so I read every etiquette book in every era and culture that I can find; some of it I agree with and some of it I do not. Society is evolving and becoming more modern, and I start creating my own thoughts and lessons through my own experiences that years later I still find myself teaching. I feel more and more empowered through education.

Eventually I enroll in a Swiss finishing school, noted by many as "the last real finishing school in Europe," where they promise to dive into every topic imaginable, from how to cut a banana with a knife and fork to how to address foreign dignitaries. (This is a far cry from my beloved college days at the University of Florida.) I am only introduced to my other thirty or so female peers by their first names, so that if someone has a title such as Princess, they are not treated differently or given privilege. I sign a contract that says I cannot reveal what happens at the school as a matter of strict confidence, which I loyally sign. I absolutely love it, and if it were not for Marco back in London, I would have tried to mop the floors to stay enrolled longer.

My Transformation Story

Broke and happily educated, I find a job at a global communications firm in London. I work almost half a decade here, climbing my way up to Senior Director, and begin to specialize in major fashion, luxury, and lifestyle American companies who are launching outside of the US for the first time. I spend a decent amount of time teaching my American clients about British and European culture, from how many times you kiss on each cheek when being greeted, to basic cultural differences in each market. I love sharing my newfound knowledge and try to teach them in the least intimidating way I know how. When I see their confidence after, I love how it makes not only them, but me feel.

One day, a client calls me in a panic, saying the CEO of their fashion company had donated to a UK charity and was invited to meet the Queen. "What does she do? How does she curtsy? What does she wear? How should she address the Queen? No photos, right?" My client explains that they tried to find British, European, or even general international protocol training in their US state without any luck whatsoever. I reassure my client that they are in good hands, and spend the next day prepping information for them. It was later that week that my client uttered the words nobody ever wants to hear: "You know, in all the years you have worked with us, we've never seen you so passionate before." At first it bothered me that my client essentially told me I was not passionate about my current job, but I now call that my "aha!" moment. I kept thinking about them not being able to find more international etiquette training in their state and that they had to fly about six thousand miles to learn it. Just as people import products into other countries, why couldn't I import this skillset as a service? I decided it would be my goal to start an international etiquette consultancy.

Almost everyone I told assured me that my idea was crazy. Most people asked me what my "plan b" was. My answer was always unwavering and clear. "I don't have a plan b, because if I make one, I will fall back on it." (I've called this my "plan b mentality" ever since.) At this point, things start moving pretty fast. I sit at my desk at work but can't think of anything else but company names and what I can teach. I decide on Beaumont Etiquette because I hear the word "beaumont" in London used socially to mean "elegantly over the top." "The meal was sooo beaumont," or even "He was so beaumont!" I love it and instantly know that I want someone to be Beaumont-educated. I feel like I'm bursting with excitement every time I think about my idea.

I launch my company in Kensington, London in 2013, the same year Marco and I are married. I take small projects I received through word of mouth, mostly teaching foreigners or expat groups living in London how to navigate British dining and culture. I instruct at nights after my regular work day. At first, I do it all for free, just for the experience to speak in front of a group. People always say you never work a day when you do what you love, and even though my pockets are empty, I leave each course feeling as though I won the lottery. As word continues to spread about my courses throughout London, I have to start taking a day here or there of "holiday" off of work in order to take on these projects. Before I know it, I am out of vacation days. I wake up every day like a small child excited to get out the door to play, and so happy that people are finding my courses helpful and referring me to others. I finally quit my job to focus on Beaumont Etiquette full time. I'm scared out of my mind of failure but do it anyway.

As chance would have it, Marco was transferred to a new job in New York City in the fall of that same year. I had no idea if my little company was going to survive America. People in Europe cared about manners and etiquette as much as they cared for just about anything else, but would it be the same in the states? I realize that if I can convince Americans that etiquette is so much more than which fork and knife to hold, they will see the great need for it, too. I know I need to teach people to think about it differently, that it's not old-fashioned, but instead a skillset that some of the most successful people globally know and practice every day. It's like the secret weapon the most charming people on earth use, and it's only now that we're figuring that out. By learning etiquette, you learn to have confidence in any situation, and who wouldn't want more confidence? Imagine walking into a networking event and leaving with ten new contacts, attending a formal dinner party and leaving the belle of the ball with multiple dinner invitations, or going to a social event and being the most coveted person in the room to speak to. These are all things that can be achieved through learning to master social interaction, from starting a conversation and keeping it going, to reading social cues and mastering charisma in any situation. It's learning to relate to people, which is emotional intelligence. This is all a part of etiquette, and it *can* be taught. I realize that, just like myself, there are millions of educated people who *know* they still have a lot to learn when it comes to etiquette, and just don't know where to go or how to learn it. It's that feeling of sitting around a table at a nice restaurant and looking down at your place setting and feeling a bit overwhelmed. It's almost like you *think* you know which fork to use, but you pause for just that slight moment to look across at the other diners to see which fork they pick up to make sure you were right. Almost everyone can relate. I think to myself that if there was some way I could "bottle" the feeling of self-assurance and give it to others, how impactful that could be, so I soon start creating course outlines with the goal of teaching confidence in social skills, dining, business, and beyond. I recognize through this new way of thinking about (and teaching) etiquette, that I can recreate interest in the states. I remember the surge of excitement and energy to get started and feeling more passionate about this than anything else I've ever put my mind to. I know this is my calling and my purpose, but I also know I have my work cut out for me!

I relaunch Beaumont Etiquette in Manhattan on October 1st of 2014. I can't afford my own office, so I set up shop in my apartment with Marco. He is supportive and exceptionally patient with me and the piles of papers and tarnished silver I'm in the process of polishing for my future dining courses. I am the proud janitor and CEO of my New York LLC. For twenty-six days, I sit at my desk during my "office hours" and do not receive one phone call or email. I stare at the phone and research companies that may need my services. I send dozens upon dozens of emails and make endless cold calls. I do not get one single booking. People tell me their employees would not be interested in "this type of thing" and some even laugh when I suggest a group training class. I do a media audit for etiquette to find that there are only approximately a half-dozen or so recent articles, mostly about cell phone etiquette in major publications, and that perhaps it was not a topic of interest in the US anymore after all. I know I must somehow change this and bring attention to this beautiful industry, and fast.

Winston Churchill had a famous quote that hung over the bar of my favorite neighborhood pub in London (The Churchill Arms) that read "Success is going from failure to failure with enthusiasm." I keep it printed on a piece of paper on my desk, and it remains one of my biggest pieces of inspiration to date. I realize I must change "tack" as the sailors say (change direction of the sail to catch wind to keep sailing) and try as many things as I can to get my business going. I have always believed in the power of positivity and that there is always a lesson to be learned and a silver lining to be seen, and between that and faith, I just kept going. I read stories of those who "failed" time and time again, my favorite being that of Mr. Dyson, the man who invented arguably the most famous vacuum on earth. He went into bankruptcy twenty-two times before he developed his first marketable prototype. It is said that in the end, he owned more land in the UK than the Queen of England.

I suspect that just like myself, there must be others in our beautiful yet casual culture who want to learn these lessons, but by initially calling my classes "manners" or "etiquette" classes, people were not receptive. I now understand that my courses are like therapy in the 90s; there is a stigma. People were slightly embarrassed to admit that they wanted to go, but knew they needed it. I know I must find a way to show that my courses are high energy, fun, and modern. I know I must get creative. I pair my syllabi with pop culture topics, and after a few free group sessions to get feedback (that I practically begged friends of friends to attend), slowly word began to travel like a tiny ripple in a lake. I now know that a tiny ripple can make it a very long way. One friend tells a freelance journalist friend about a course I created called "The Duchess Effect" (*not* an etiquette class!) where they can learn the "style, grace and poise of a Duchess." I get a call from this journalist saying she'd like to take my course and write about her experience in *Vogue* magazine. By the grace of my Champagne angels, she loves it and reviews it with gold stars. Some call it luck, but I do not believe in luck (luck is when "preparation meets opportunity," as Oprah says). The Duke and Duchess of Cambridge announce they would be flying into New York for their first visit just two weeks later, which aligns perfectly with my article debut. I receive just over 1,500 emails, phone calls, and newsletter subscriptions in forty-eight hours. I know I am onto something. I soon can finally afford a small (very small) New York office.

I write down what my "dream" next steps are for my company and visualize it daily. Most people are afraid to go straight to the dream, so they start small and build confidence, leaving all the big dreams open and accessible for the brave ones. I decide not to start small, and instead go straight to the dream. This leads me to pitch my idea for a modern-day adult finishing program to The Plaza Hotel, the castle-like building in Manhattan overlooking Central Park and Fifth Avenue that while growing up I only saw in movies or read about in books. I ask around until I find a contact, which eventually leads me to a meeting with Ariana from the communications team of the hotel. I walk in the grandiose gold and marble lobby, which literally sparkles from the thousands of crystals dangling from the chandeliers overhead. Wearing a dress with a neckline of dramatic ostrich feathers, I begin to paint the picture. I tell her we are about to create a renaissance of manners in America and bring modern etiquette to younger generations. I pitch to the hotel as if they are already on board. I tell them that it will be the go-to lifestyle program in the US. While I am projecting such confidence in my pitch, I genuinely don't know if anyone will enroll. I get a phone call from Ari the next month saying they have agreed to partner and plan to launch the program the following year. It's as if every Christmas for my entire life came all at once. I hang up the phone and while I try to catch my breath realize that I now must deliver.

I spend my days with the internal team at The Plaza learning about secret rooms and staircases in the hotel. I spend my early mornings picking out silver and china for our courses, and my evenings standing in the grand ballroom practicing addressing the imaginary crowd. There are logistics for days that I never dreamed there would be, but I am so excited that I don't feel the least bit overwhelmed. I remind myself daily how grateful I am for this chance and it charges me for the following day.

Around this time I also find out the joyful news that I am pregnant with a baby girl. Marco and I are over the moon, but everyone tells me stress is bad for the baby and to take it easy. I remind them this is not stress at all, that in fact it's the most exciting thing that has ever happened to my career and I'm giddy with delight. As the excitement around the program grows within the hotel and New York, I soon realize I am out of my league with the amount of work to be done and need a business partner. I think long and hard about who this should be and I think of Anne, who is a true New Yorker, a part-time journalist, and mom of two. I first met Anne when she interviewed me for an article on royal etiquette for *The Huffington Post* the year before. After the interview was done, we stayed after talking for hours about our love of everything royal and British. We clicked instantly. Anne is brilliant, a good friend, and a won't-take-no-for-an-answer girl from Brooklyn.

We meet for a coffee and I admire her glittery Chanel boots paired with jeans as she walks in. She plops down into the seat and opens her notebook to a blank page, pulls out her pen, and says, "Talk to me." Without sugarcoating a single detail, I tell her my idea to start the first finishing program of its kind in America at The Plaza Hotel. I not only tell her my plan and that I have no money to invest upfront, but that I want to know if she wants to be my partner and run it. She silently stares back at me across the table as if I have snakes coming out of my hair and reminds me that she has never taken an etiquette class in her life. I explain that it will require hundreds of hours of work, and we'll only get paid if people book. "So, there is a chance we work for months to launch, and nobody buys a single ticket and we make no money?" I nod my head yes. Then, complete silence. Eyes wide and processing, she finally says "Love it. I'm in!"

With that, I have my first Beaumont team member, who eventually becomes my partner. I adore Anne because she is fearless. She is the tech-savvy organizer, and I am the creative, but we are equally big dreamers. We are polar opposites but find ourselves laughing for hours on end over my growing belly and teacups. We spend long nights building websites and writing copy, and up to our ears in budgets and Excel spreadsheets, but we love every minute of it. We spend day and night at The Plaza and the staff soon recognize us as a part of the team. Now that Anne is on board, I can barely think of how I would do it without her. In fact, the day before I went into labor, I was working with Anne and Ari at The Plaza. At this point, I was almost ten days overdue and looked as though I would pop at any moment. "A Plaza baby birth, Mrs. Meier?" the doormen joked with me.

On November 23, 2016 my little Valentina LeMont (LeMont is a beautiful village in Switzerland) Meier was born. I spent the rest of the year at home, and with Marco couriering my work back and forth for me to Anne and The Plaza. When the baby was asleep, instead of sleeping myself I couldn't wait to get to work. Holding the baby in my left arm, I type one handed on my computer with my right. I work harder than I ever have before, often one eye open reading Valentina my course outlines as if they were lullabies while covered in baby who-knows-what. We launch The Plaza Hotel Finishing Program with Beaumont Etiquette in January of 2017. The media go wild and we sell out of almost every course within forty-eight hours of the *Town and Country* press announcement. The launch of our etiquette program is covered internationally in media in over two hundred news outlets within months. There is such demand, we double our classes and even add children and teen etiquette courses, all which sell out again. I am over the moon not just that we're "doing it" but more that we have helped convince people that etiquette is still relevant, I argue, more so than ever. "It's trending" someone tells me, but that word bothers me, as I want it to stay as a classic cultural staple and not just a fad.

I spend the next chapter of my life that year teaching thousands of people from all over the world how to be polished to perfection, how to be the most charming person in the room, how to dress elegantly, how to navigate an eight course meal, and how to change their vocabulary overnight to what I call "sophisticated verbiage." Most importantly, I start out every course by telling people that the root of what they are learning is kindness and respect, creating a powerful army of nice people. My dream of instilling confidence through etiquette is no longer just a dream.

Like a game of telephone, chatter starts to spread, and I soon find that I am the person behind the scenes teaching some of the world's most recognized socialites and celebrities. I'm asked to sign countless NDAs and privacy contracts, and am flown to some of America's greatest private mansions where I discreetly instruct, primp, and polish family members to perfection. I have to practice keeping a straight face when I walk into a client's home as if to show no emotion in recognizing them, even if I just read about their most recent drama that same week in *People* magazine. I receive inquiries by royal families and politicians around the world, and find myself in dizzying and exciting new territory. One day we get a call to be the official etiquette partners for British sensation *The Downton Abbey Exhibition* that is touring America. I take the meeting via Skype call from the neck up, with Valentina happily strapped to my chest.

I finally, for the first time in my life, feel like I have found my purpose and that maybe, just maybe, my passion will leave a mark of good on this planet after all. From unpolished, small-town girl to being named "The Queen of Etiquette" by the world's most read newspaper, *The Daily Mail* (I can't believe my eyes when the feature lands on my desk), my social "transformation" experiment appeared to work. So, can anyone make a life-changing transformation? Absolutely. I, the girl who at one time only owned flip-flops, who ten years later was serving Prince Charles a gin and tonic on a silver tray in the famous Astley House on Hyde Park near Buckingham Palace (I almost fainted, literally speaking), am living proof.

I know it's not possible for everyone to travel to New York City to take our courses, so it became my next goal to share my knowledge through a book (*oh, hello there!*) with anyone who wished to learn to become the best, most polished, and kind versions of themselves. It's true that you must know the rules to break them, and I want everyone to know how! Through practical lessons, a bit of humor, some Myka-isms, and a few slices of humble pie, I have put together this easy-to-follow guide to becoming overall more poised and polished. If I can make the transformation, just about anyone can.

Chapter 2

Turning Heads

How to Create the Best First Impression

Now that you know my transformation story, it's time to get started on your own. Hopefully it gave you the courage, motivation, or inspiration you needed to start creating the life you always dreamed of. And while it's up to you, and only you, to make these changes, this guide will keep you on track. To "transform" is the first step of the five included in the Meier Method. In my opinion, it is the most important, as it's the foundation for the other four steps. Once you undergo your transformation (step 1), you will attract (step 2) the people and the life you want. Next, you will learn how to empower (step 3) yourself and others, and not be afraid to go after the things you always wanted to achieve. Then, you are ready to thrive (step 4) in your environment so no matter if it's a casual networking event or a formal dinner party, you'll know how to dress, who to talk to, what to talk about, and which of those four knives to pick up first. Last, you will put everything into practice (step 5) and start living and enjoying your new life. The Five-Step Meier Method will help you craft the life you want and give you the confidence to pursue it, all with the core training being, you guessed it, etiquette.

Let's be honest, everyone wants to make not just a good, but an incredible first impression. Who doesn't want to be the life of the party, the belle of the ball, or the new superstar at work? Now, it's said that you have seven seconds or less to make a first impression. While it may seem unfair to be "judged" in seven seconds, that's just how fast the human brain observes and processes details about someone else. I actually think that if we know *what* people are observing during these seven seconds, then we also know *how* to control any situation. Easy, right? I'd be much more worried if we had thirty minutes to make a first impression—that's much harder! Instead, lets embrace the fact that we only have to pull it together for seven seconds. Let me therefore introduce you to my "7-in-7 Theory," in which it is crucial to align seven important aspects of yourself in order to come across as the superstar you are in the first seven seconds of making an entrance. I created this theory because of the seven aspects I consistently observe that make up a first impression:

1. Physical placement
2. Facial control
3. Personal presentation
4. Posture
5. Voice
6. Body language (including eye contact)
7. Charisma

If you think it sounds overwhelming to master all of this at once, think again. If you understand what people notice about each point and why, you can learn, adjust, practice, and perfect your first impression. One thing I want to address, however, is that I've heard many times that you only have one chance to make a first impression. Here is where I agree, yet disagree. While I agree that people will make up their mind about you quite quickly, I think that every day is a new chance for a first impression. It's never too late to change the impression your social group may have about you! The next time you walk into that party to greet the same people you've known for ages is also a perfect chance to make a new impression. Remember, every day is a fresh start to make a first impression—it just happens to be the first of that day/week/month, that's all! The 7-in-7 Theory is important to acknowledge and understand, because all of these components are what help make up a first impression and they are all within our control.

Now, a little secret to share with you. Before you learn the 7-in-7, the most important question before every first impression is: *Who are you meeting*? Whenever I walk into a room, I always do my research first on who will be inside. By knowing who you are walking in to meet, and the formality of the person or group, you can plan ahead to dress and present yourself to be the most relatable and therefore likeable. This is an important step to follow, because people tend to relate best to those they share similarities with. Not always will you be able to find out the exact people you are meeting, however, and in that case, it's best to mirror either the venue, theme, or location of the event. For example, if I know my thirty clients today are all from a very corporate financial firm, I will likely wear a dark colored dress with a blazer and polished closed-toe shoes, because that's how I know they'll be dressed. Let's say the very next day, I have a group of thirty women taking an afternoon tea course at The Plaza Hotel. You'll probably catch me in ostrich feathers and oversized strands of pearls. In both cases, I will plan ahead and mirror the group's formality and brand with my appearance and presentation to be the most relatable I can to each. While you should always be yourself, it's also important to know how to be a chameleon of sorts in order to be the most relatable you can to others. Remember, trust is built on first impressions. Once you know who will be in the room you're entering, then you can tackle the 7-in-7 points that, all together, will give you the best shot at making a killer first impression!

The 7-in-7 Theory
7 THINGS TO DO IN THE FIRST 7 SECONDS OF MAKING AN ENTRANCE TO MAKE A GREAT IMPRESSION

1. Physical Placement

This point is to ensure all that hard work you put into preparing for your meeting doesn't go sour upon entering the room. When you walk into any door or room, always remember to never turn your back to the room you are entering or people you are greeting. Why? Well, we know you only have seven seconds to show that beautiful mug of yours, so why on earth would you turn your back to close the door when you enter the room? Instead, the next time you enter, walk in and open the door with your right hand. Walk through the door, and then by changing your hands behind your back, the door should then close with your left hand. That leaves your right hand open to meet and shake hands with those you are greeting. Your eye contact never has to leave those you are walking in to meet, and your chin stays parallel to the floor and confident as ever. Now, glide your gorgeous self into that room like you own it!

2. Facial Control

Are you serious? Likeable? Tense? Friendly? We immediately look to someone's face and eyes to connect with another person before looking at anything else. Without even realizing it, we are analyzing

22

the other person's face. So, what exactly are we looking for? The two most important parts are the mouth and the eyes. If you walk into a room with your eyes and mouth open, that is a sign of openness, receptiveness, and friendliness. If your mouth is closed, or even pinched, you instantly look less approachable. It sounds basic, but a smile is one of the most important indicators of friendliness and approachability, and one we often forget when we walk into a room.

3. Personal Presentation

After physically entering a room and connecting face to face with another person, the next thing people tend to notice is your appearance. How did you put yourself together, dress yourself, and ultimately present yourself? You are in charge of packaging yourself to other people, and however you choose to do so will impact the first impression you make. From this day on, I want you to *dress the way you want to be addressed*. This simply means that the way you choose to present yourself is how you will be addressed by other people. To create your own personal brand, you first need to visualize what it is that you want to present, then you need to make it happen. I will take you through easy steps on how to create your own brand in Chapter 4 (page 59). With personal presentation, there is something that can still ruin a first impression: the small details, even outside of style and grooming! One common example I can think of is when someone walks into a meeting and is dressed to the nines, then they sit down and take out a chewed pen and spiral notebook with pieces of shredded paper coming off the sides. *Eek*! They just lost me. These are the small details that can ruin a great first impression, and are some of the easiest to fix. Before you walk into any meeting, party, or event, look at all aspects of your presentation. Oh, and don't forget that your hair, skin, and nails count too when it comes to a polished presentation. I'll go over my tips on how to become instantly more polished while dressing and grooming in Chapter 4 (page 59).

4. Posture

Why is posture so important and what do we need it for? To practice good posture is essentially to demonstrate positive body language, which can show that you are attentive, alert, confident, and powerful. A large part of what you say is actually done through nonverbal body language, and not just your voice. That's why posture and carrying yourself in the right way says so much about you. You can make yourself instantly more attractive and approachable by showing through posture that you are an interested and engaged person. It's the law of attraction that you will meet others who are excited to mingle by literally positioning yourself as ready to meet and socialize. Think about it this way. You can be wearing the most incredible gown or tuxedo of your wildest dreams, but if you're slouched in the corner or standing with a curved spine, shoulders forward, or chin down, nobody is likely to approach or even notice you. You not only may appear to lack confidence, but you also don't "own" the outfit that so beautifully dresses you. Instead, the outfit "owns" you. People notice the gown or tuxedo, and not the person in it. Let's flip the switch and make sure our clothing never again takes away from the fact that we are confident, powerful, social, and ready to mingle.

The Chin

To start, there are three cornerstones of posture: chin, shoulders, and legs. One in line without the other simply will not do for excellent posture, but the chin is often the first cornerstone I like to correct to make an instant difference in the way someone is perceived. While it is fun to walk around and take photos of ourselves with

books on our heads when we think of etiquette school, it is not very practical in my opinion. I often find it actually makes people look robotic.

Make sure to roll your shoulders back, and keep your chin so that it is parallel to the floor at all times. If your chin dips too low (and I'm talking centimeters here), then you may appear that you lack confidence, are shy, or like you don't want to be in conversation. If you point your chin a little too high, then you risk looking a bit arrogant, aloof, or like you're not present. Either too low or too high can make you appear less approachable.

Sitting Posture

Posture while sitting is arguably the hardest to master, because we tend to relax after just a few minutes, curving our spines to find comfort, ultimately slouching. Nobody likes a slouch. During the next few paragraphs, practice with me as you read this.

- Avoid using arm rests. The moment you use arm rests, you slowly start to relax and your spine begins to curve.
- Your back should not be touching the back of the chair. Imagine you have about the width of a golf ball or egg from the back of your tailbone to the back of the chair. By not

leaning backward into your chair, you tend to keep a straight spine, which, when sitting, prevents you from slouching.

- You want to be sure that you are at least 1–1.5 hand's width away from a table if you have one in front of you. This simply ensures that you are not leaning or hovering over the table or desk. Imagine Princess Grace of Monaco or Frank Sinatra slouching at the table . . . just wouldn't happen, would it?!

- Remember, no elbows on the table . . . ever. Not at a desk, dinner table, or boardroom. Instead, try resting your forearms on the table, but only if there is no food coming to the table. More on what to do with your hands and arms during meals in the dining chapter (page 105).

While I love teaching modern etiquette in a gender-neutral way, for anatomical reasons on this next lesson, I would suggest the below options for sitting.

Gents

Gentlemen, try placing your legs hip-width apart and heels firmly planted on the floor. If you cross your legs, you may do so at the knee, but you simply want to watch that the bottom of your shoe faces down and not to the people you are interacting with, because no matter how beautifully polished your shoe is, the moment you stepped in florescent green gum on the way up the stairs to your meeting, the gum on your sole is what we may see.

Ladies

I recommend keeping your knees and ankles together. If you wish to cross your legs, you have a few options. The below sitting positions

Queen's pose

Duchess slant

Cambridge cross

Sussex slant

have been long practiced by some of the most elegant and powerful women on earth, so I was inspired to create names for them after the British Royal Family. If you're a little shorter in stature, inch to the end of the seat of the chair and try the Queen's pose.

Standing Posture

People often think that posture is only when you are sitting, but it's actually important to practice while you are also standing, walking (especially if wearing heels), getting in and out of a car, descending a staircase, standing still, or even taking a photo. If you are standing, you should have a slight curve of your spine inward so that your shoulders and your bum are the two parts touching a wall if you were to stand against it. Here are three pose options to try that demonstrate excellent posture while standing still or taking a photo:

Sussex Stance

Exhibited by The Duchess of Sussex during countless photos, and also while standing to speak, notice the chin is parallel to the floor, hands gently relaxed to the side (not clenched) and shoulders rolled back. Legs are together and one foot crosses over the other with toes pointed toward the camera. Keeping your body in a cylindrical shape elongates your body, and notice there is no hand on hip with an oddly angled elbow jut-

ting out. Often taking a photo straight-on may not be your most flattering position, so feel free to keep your feet planted and turn your body slightly to the angle you prefer toward the camera, toes always pointing to the lens.

Cambridge Carry

Often exhibited by The Duchess of Cambridge, the toes are aligned, and shoulders are rolled back, but hands are in front of the body. Instead of clenching fists or intertwining fingers together, which sometimes can make you look tense, she is often holding a handbag in front of her. Holding a handbag, tablet, notebook, etc. is a good solution for those who never know what to do with their hands.

Duke Demeanor

The Duke of Cambridge absolutely knocks it out of the park with his posture, always looking poised yet powerful. The common go-to we often observe him practicing is standing tall, feet firmly planted side by side, and his hands in what I call a double clasp (notice the fingers are not intertwined but instead one hand is over the top of the other hand with the back of both hands facing the camera and fingers out of view).

Staircase Posture

Posture is key here. Think how many staircases you have walked down in your life. Stairs are typically all the same for the most part, equal distance from one to the next, measuring about 7.5 inches high per standard stair step in the US. Besides looking down at the first and last two steps to gauge distance and step height, you don't need to look down at the steps as you're walking. Many staircases serve as the grand entrance into a building, party, or home, and are very often the first place someone will see you, so you want to keep your eyes up toward the room and not looking down step for step. Instead, use the banister as your guide (you don't need to grip it, but just gently rest your open hand on it and slide it along as you walk). Walk nice and slow so you don't stumble or trip. I like to repeat the word *glide* in my head as I walk down a staircase. Try not to bounce and instead imagine you are gliding down a staircase on air, softly and elegantly into the room.

If you are walking down a staircase with a dress or skirt, angle your body so that your toes are slightly pointing toward the banister. By angling your feet so that your toes are in the direction of the banister, it will protect your modesty when walking down a staircase with a curvature to it, so people standing at the bottom can't see up your dress or skirt. If you are walking down with trousers, simply point toes forward and rest your right hand on the banister or railing while slowly stepping down. Make sure to keep your chin parallel and eyes up. It's a nice gesture if you are not wearing heels to walk down one step in front of anyone who is, and to lend your hand for them to hold if needed. We often saw President Kennedy do this with First Lady Jackie while walking down steps.

Walking Posture

We tend to think that while in motion we don't need to practice good posture, which is totally false. Think about how many times you make an entrance by walking into a room. How does one achieve grace? Remember to walk gracefully and with intention, and slow down! By slowing down, you will have less of a bounce each time you step, which you want to avoid. This means your speed, your arm swing, and all. Think of the most graceful person in your head. You wouldn't see them running down Fifth Avenue looking manic.

Now, walking in heels is a whole other ballgame. When you see someone walking awkwardly in heels, it's usually caused by one of three things: A. the heel and/or platform is too high; B. the shoe doesn't fit correctly; or C. they don't have practice. Walking in heels is completely different than walking in flat shoes, whether they be sneakers, loafers, or ballet flats. When walking in flats, it's fine to walk hip-width apart. When walking in heels, however, you want to

adjust so that you are subtly walking more one foot in front of the other. If you have nothing in your hands, rest them gently to your sides, fingers loosely open. If you have something in your hands, such as a clutch or folder, hold either to one side with one hand or in front of you with both hands. While a little back-and-forth movement of your arms is natural, avoid swinging your arms.

Getting in and out of a Car

Getting in and out of a car takes practice, but once you master it, you're set to always look graceful while doing so. It isn't always easy, especially if wearing a dress or skirt. For gentlemen, it's more about taking your time and stepping out one foot at a time. I am delighted to teach you a Meier Method I created and coined the "Swivel-and-Pop." I recommend using this method when wearing something like a dress, skirt, or wispy top where you may flash those awaiting your arrival.

When getting out of a car using the Swivel-and-Pop, you first want to make sure that you are sitting closest to the door you will be getting out of, and scoot your bum as close to the edge of the

seat as possible. You don't want to have to slide across a seat to make an exit. When the door opens, whether you open it yourself or there is a doorman helping you, this is where a little upper body strength comes in. Using your arms and a little core strength, keep your knees and ankles together at all times while lifting yourself up slightly with both arms and at the same time swiveling your body so that your

legs, while staying together, turn out of the car. Once your feet hit the ground, use both of your arms again to lift yourself or "pop" out of the car—hence the name Swivel-and-Pop. If you have a handbag, leave it to the side of your seat and, once out of the car, gently reach in after it.

Getting back into a car is easier and almost the same process. The door opens, and you turn your backside toward the seat. Lower yourself into the seat. Once your bum hits the seat, while keeping your knees and ankles together, place both hands on the seat and swivel your legs back into the car.

5. Voice

Now that you look great, have powerful posture, are practicing positive body language, and know how to make an entrance, you feel like you must be set, right? Well, even with all those things on point, imagine walking into a room looking amazing and poised but when you open your mouth to speak, your voice doesn't match the rest of the package. You almost had them convinced! It is easy to fix, however, and having a strong voice is key in having a strong presence. Your voice is the number one way to show lack of confidence and authority outside of posture. Imagine I am the head of an organization, and I walk into a room to lead a meeting and I sit down, and the first words that come out of my mouth are soft and monotone. I'm cringing just thinking about it! Just like that, you've taken your level of authority down a notch. In order to make a powerful first impression, you must ensure your voice matches your personal presentation. There are four parts to every person's voice—which are called the "4 P's," which is a vocal training method developed by Diana Mather, author of *Body Language Secrets*, and they stand for Pitch, Pace, Pause, and Passion. Unless you are a professional public speaker, everyone has one to work on.

Pitch

This P is the most common of the four to work on. Is your voice showing emotion or are you monotone? You should have two points of inflection in every sentence to engage people in what you are saying. Without enthusiasm in your voice, good luck trying to sell anything to anyone, let alone yourself when making a first impression! Another pitch issue is that of being either too loud, too soft, or making your voice go up at the end of your sentences. Sound familiar? Don't worry, it's fixable!

Pace

Do you get so excited about an idea that you speak too fast? Well, sadly for you, speaking fast can also be a sign of nervousness that shows a lack of poise and confidence. We must learn to slow down. Is your voice the opposite and too slow? Much more graceful a problem, but too slow can be a bore and lose interest in others.

Pause

Do you ask questions without waiting until others answer before you start talking over them? This can be one of the most frustrating P's for others because they can never get two words in. We want to ensure you are speaking in a way that allows for conversation back and forth and that you're also not just talking without pausing to let others speak.

Passion

Without passion in your voice, people may lose interest. Passion is something we all need when we are speaking professionally, socially, or when talking about a subject important to us.

Think about which P you need to work on—pitch, pace, pause, or passion—and start working to correct your voice to become more powerful. Now, what comes out of your mouth is another chapter entirely! We'll work on your charisma and attitude in Chapter 5 (page 75).

6. Body Language (Including Eye Contact)

According to a *New York Times* article, *The Definitive Book of Body Language* (Sept. 24, 2006), Albert Mehrabian, a pioneer researcher of body language in the 1950s, found that the total impact of a message is about 7 percent verbal (words only) and 38 percent vocal (including tone of voice, inflection, and other sounds) and 55 percent nonverbal. Just think about that—you could say one thing but if your body and facial expression say something else, you're not getting the message across. Make sure with your first impression that your body language is open, approachable, and likeable.

First lesson: put that phone away! It's like a social safety net, but when you first enter a room, to look most friendly and approachable, make sure you are not looking down at your phone and instead directly at the people you are approaching. When you meet someone, you're not just maintaining eye contact during the initial handshake, but also after you put your hand down and while you are still speaking. Have you ever had someone look over your shoulder at someone else while speaking to you or shaking your hand? It's almost like you want to stop and say, "Umm . . . would you like me to introduce you to her instead?!" Tsk-tsk.

Did you also know that there is an exact eye to look into when you want to come across as likable versus authoritative? I'll teach you all my tips and party tricks on how to read and react to body language in Chapter 6 (page 82). Often people tell me they feel awkward "locking" eyes when conversing with people they don't know. Here's the trick to help it feel more natural: When someone is speaking, always make direct eye contact with them the entire time. When you are speaking, you can take quick breaks from direct eye contact and look up or down as you are thinking and speaking, but always go back to their eyes after your "thinking" eye movement.

Another aspect of body language is nodding your head when you are not speaking. To be in a conversation and blankly staring at someone isn't showing that you are comprehending. Instead, while other people are speaking, make sure to nod to acknowledge you understand or are listening.

7. Charisma

Think about what makes someone attractive. I didn't say pretty, or handsome, but attractive. What makes you want to talk to someone, learn more about them, spend time with them? It's hugely their energy, but also about how they make you feel. I find people with charisma tend to have high emotional intelligence and good etiquette. They put others first, always complimenting, making an effort to connect and build rapport with other people. Many people say one is just born with a charismatic nature, but I don't agree. I think charisma, or charm, as people call it, can be learned, practiced, and mastered. I feel so strongly about projecting positive energy and charisma that I have dedicated an entire how-to section on achieving it in this book.

So, there you have it. The 7-in-7 theory on how to make the best first impression through seven steps. It's only the first part of the Meier Method, but you need this foundation before moving on.

Chapter 3

What Would Jackie Say?

Personal Presentation to Sophisticated Dressing and Grooming

Myka-ism: "The only drama a lady should bring is through her outfit."

Myka-ism: "A gentleman is defined not by the polish of his shoes, but by the time he took to polish his shoes."

Believe it or not, having a strong presence doesn't require an outgoing personality. A person who is more on the quiet side can still have a grand presence. Having a presence means that people notice you. People with a strong presence make it known when they enter a room, almost as if the energy shifts, causing heads to turn and notice. This chapter will be your guide on how to achieve presence so that when those doors open, heads will turn—and for all the right reasons. There is an artform to this, as heads can turn when you're too loud, which may work against you. That's not the goal. You don't want to demand attention; you simply want people to notice you because you have such a strong presence. See the difference? Let's start with when you first enter a room. This can cause people to feel anxious, but really once you know the following key introductions and greetings, you will be able to glide in with no issues whatsoever. I've got you. Here is my quick guide to meetings, greetings, and introductions.

Meetings and Greetings

To help when you are meeting people for the first time, I created a Meier Method called the HACH (**H**andshake, **A**ir kiss, **C**heek kiss, **H**ug) system of greetings. Outside of this system, there are no other formal styles I recommend you follow in the Western world. The only exception would be when greeting a royal, but that's a whole other book!

The Handshake

When in doubt, go with the handshake. Yes, it's seen as formal, but it is also a sign of respect. I personally am a hugger, but we must be conscious of people's preference of personal space and recognize that not everyone is comfortable with touching outside of a hand. Always remember that your handshake is your physical signature and that the way you shake a hand can say a lot about you.

Rules of the handshake

Right-to-right, web-to-web: Extend your right hand to shake the other person's right hand. Open your hand angled at about 30 degrees so that the web of your hand meets the web of the other person's hand.

Strength: You should squeeze the other person's hand so that it comes across as firm and assertive, yet never aggressive. Many women I meet say they were taught to shake hands softly, but in modern etiquette, especially professionally, this is no longer appropriate and can show weakness or lack of confidence. Not on my watch, ladies! No dead fish handshakes here. Regardless of gender, you never want to shake a hand by squeezing too strongly so it causes discomfort to the other person.

Power play: When shaking hands, some people put one hand over the top of other person's hand. I often hear people say they think it is a sign of warmth, but it is actually a sign of power. Unless you are trying to assert authority over another person, I advise you not to do this.

Length: In business, we shake using two pumps of the hand, elbow in. In social situations, we shake hands using three pumps. This is because in business we get straight to the point with two pumps, but socially we often have a little bit more to talk about. Now, if you get caught locked in a handshake with what I call an "over-shaker" don't fear . . . just go with it. It's unfortunate for the upper wobbly bits of your arm, but it will be over soon, don't worry. Pulling away otherwise may be highly offensive to the person you are shaking hands with.

The Air Kiss

The air kiss is what we do socially. It is when we lean in and put our right cheek to the other person's right cheek. We do touch cheeks, but very gently. Our actual lips never touch the skin of the other person's cheek. No loud "muuuuahhhh" noises either, and don't lean in without touching cheeks, as it can look disingenuous to kiss the air. Another common mistake? Standing straight up like a tin solider, leaning in, and popping back. Instead, when you lean in, take your right hand and gently place it on the other person's right elbow or the outside of their forearm. This also helps you determine if someone is coming in for a second kiss. Remember that we always follow the etiquette and customs of the country and culture we are in. This means you must know how many kisses are appropriate in each country, as it can vary slightly. For example, in the United States we offer one kiss, right cheek to right cheek. In the United Kingdom, we offer two kisses, starting first with one kiss on the right cheek, then one kiss on the left cheek. In other countries in Europe, such as Switzerland for example, we offer three kisses. One kiss on the right cheek, one on the left, and a third on the right cheek again.

The Cheek Kiss

This is reserved for close friends, family, and children. The cheek kiss is often incorrectly practiced in public at social events. Think about when you see a man dressed beautifully at a wedding and then notice red lips on his cheek—eek! This should never happen. The cheek kiss is when the lips actually touch the cheek of the person we are kissing. All other rules of the air kiss still apply otherwise.

The Hug

Very similar to the cheek kiss, the hug is also only reserved for close friends, family, and children.

Introductions

When introducing people, there are three "orders of introduction" that should be followed to show respect. Anyone who knows these rules might be highly offended if introduced incorrectly. Decades ago, the lady's name was always said first in an introduction, but etiquette is becoming less gender-specific and more gender-neutral so this is no longer the case. When you are trying to decide who to introduce first, think to yourself, *who do I want to show respect to first?*

The three orders of introductions are as follows:

1. Most VIP person in the room is introduced first (President Smith, may I please introduce you to Vice President Craft.).
2. A more senior person is introduced first (Grandpa, may I please introduce you to my friend Frank.).

3. If everyone in the room is the same status, introduce people by saying the woman's name first, followed by the man's name (Suzanne, may I please introduce you to Nicholas.). If all of the above stand in the same room, simply say the name of the person you want to honor first, and rarely will you ever go wrong.

Never mirror introduce. Why don't you want to say, "Meghan, may I please introduce you to Harry. Harry, please meet Meghan"? Because you want to give the two people you are introducing something to talk about straightaway. Instead, I would say, "Meghan, may I please introduce you to Harry. Harry just moved into the neighborhood, and Meghan has been living here for the past two years, and is even the captain of the local tennis team." You essentially want to give them something to talk about and start a conversation. Otherwise, they will probably just say, "Very nice to meet you," and are left in an awkward position not knowing where to go from there. If you are introducing one person to a group of people, start with the VIP person first and introduce to everyone else. "Dr. Vera, may I please introduce you to Larisa, Robert, Anthony and Roman." The expression "may I please" is the correct formal way to introduce people.

Polished Dressing and Grooming

My grandmother taught me firsthand that just because someone has money does not mean they have class, and that always stuck with me. She also taught me that no matter your budget, look for investment pieces that are good quality, not littered with logos, made with cheap fabric, or too trendy. No matter where your starting point is in your transformation, try to keep one important thing in mind: dress for the position you want, not the one you are in.

You Are a Brand

From this day forward I want you to start thinking of yourself as a brand. When we think of a brand, we often think of things like our favorite electronic device, lipstick, or shoe brand. You, however, are a walking, breathing billboard of a brand. You are in charge of positioning and marketing yourself, so what does your brand say about you? Would you buy it? Would you aspire to it? If not, then nobody else will either.

I remember being in college and going to buy my mom a birthday gift at a fancy store in the mall. I really wanted something special, and had saved up for a nice piece of jewelry. I already knew what I wanted, but as I stood at the not-so-busy counter, I noticed that all of the other people standing there were getting served before me, even if I had been waiting (obviously!) longer. I watched in disbelief as the saleswoman glanced over at me and then ignored me. I patiently waited and then moved closer to her and then even closer until I was directly in front of her and she could no longer ignore me. I did eventually get served, but I left thinking about why that happened. On my drive home I realized that I had walked into a very expensive store, and was wearing a grungy looking outfit with messy hair. I had branded myself as if I didn't care so therefore she didn't care either. Now, it was horrible etiquette for her to have harshly judged me and unfairly ignored me, but I realize now that I didn't position myself as the brand I wanted to represent. I call this my "pretty woman" or "aha" moment. I wanted to dress up and walk back in there and show her (I didn't), but I also knew that I was partly to blame for not looking as though I respected myself. By dressing yourself in a respectful manner, you are showing respect to others. From that day forward I decided it was important to mirror the effort of the person I was meeting. I've never again had a pretty woman moment. One of my favorite quotes is "Dress the way you want to be addressed." I live by this now and advise my clients to do the same.

If you have ever taken my social etiquette and style course, you probably have what I call a "Branding Board" at home. This is an exercise that may sound time-consuming but is incredibly worth it, and even quite fun. A branding board is a collage of photos that you put together, either electronically or by cutting out actual magazine photos and gluing them onto paper. You want to cut out looks you love that inspire you, but are also achievable. This tangible visualization of your brand can evolve and change as and when you wish. You can keep it on your phone or if it's a physical branding board you can hang it in the back of your closet. Every time you get dressed, ask yourself, "Would this photo fit on my branding board?" I started practicing the branding board exercise when I moved back to New York from London. I had just started pitching companies my etiquette services and got a big lead when I met a man in my building mailroom who was the CEO of a major fashion label in New York City. He asked me to pitch to his team to teach them, and I went dressed to the nines to present. I looked polished, on-brand, and felt powerful. I left the building feeling it went extremely well. I wrote the CEO a thank-you email and spent the rest of the night thinking I might have just landed my first major corporate client. The next morning, I woke up at 5:30 a.m. with a killer sore throat. I rolled out of bed and put on a sweater over my pajama pants (it was only 6 a.m. by now and I knew nobody was awake yet to see me out and about) and decided to quickly run downstairs to the convenience store on my block for some medicine. I was in line to pay, my hair up in a ponytail drooping off my head, when I heard

"Myka?" I cringed, shrugged my shoulders to my ears, and slowly turned around to see the CEO of the company I had presented to only fifteen hours earlier. He was immaculately dressed as he was the day before and heading off to work. The polished woman who just told him she could primp and polish his retail team to perfection, stood looking like a character out of *Night of the Living Dead*. No matter what fumbling excuse came out of my mouth, it didn't matter. I never heard from him again. The lesson I learned here is that I wasn't living my brand. From that day forward I knew I needed to eat, sleep, and live my brand to permanently become my brand. I realized that if you only become "on brand" on special occasions, it will never truly feel natural.

Learn from me, and the next time you think you'll just quickly run over to the store in your sweatpants to pick up some shampoo, think again. It's Murphy's Law. That's the exact moment you will see your future date, friend, or boss. It all goes back to being prepared for anything that comes your way.

How to Look and Feel W-O-W

Years ago, I started "dressing in theme." This means that when you go to a party, an event, a cocktail hour, or even just to work, dress for the place you are going and the environment you will be in. Now, dressing in theme does not mean wearing a costume; think more festive and fun for the occasion. If I'm going to a summer garden party, for instance, I may be in colorful flowy fabrics with an amazing pair of bright floral earrings. The secret of someone with great style is to dress like you had a ball getting ready that day—it truly shows. If you are wearing a dull outfit, you will look and feel dull. Try to have fun while picking out your clothing and getting ready! Put on your favorite song, you know, the one that when it comes on makes you want to dance (mine is Whitney Houston's

"How Will I Know"). Not only are you setting the mood to your day or evening, but by dressing with this mentality, you appear happier (and remember, the most charismatic people are the happiest, and happy people are the most attractive)! The goal is to have a sophisticated and elegant look with a twist of fun. That means to always add *one* thing to your body that pops out. If I'm wearing all black, I'll add a wow pair of leopard heels, a beret, or an amazing blazer with big gold buttons. This one piece can be an accessory or part of your outfit. After you get dressed, look in the mirror and identify what your one "wow" piece is.

Right-Hand Ring

It's very hard to dress fabulously when you are feeling not-so-wow. This, my lovelies, is the vicious cycle of personal presentation. You don't feel good, so you throw on whatever is easiest, but then when you leave the house you end up *acting* like you are dressed how you feel . . . like poo! To counteract this, try putting on the most incredible thing you own. This is a perfect time to introduce you to my "right-hand ring" mentality. On days where I wake up and nothing fits (or looks good), this is what you do. Find one thing that you can put on that makes you feel amazing. Your item should be something that will always fit no matter what fluctuations your body goes through. It could be a great tie, a nice pair of shoes, a pair of earrings, that amazing color lipstick. Once you identify what this item is, it becomes your go-to wow factor. On the days you wake up and the clouds are following your every move, take out this piece and put it on. Now, such a fabulous piece could only be worn by a fabulous person. Therefore, as soon as you put it on, you must do that stunning piece justice by instantly becoming the confident owner.

My go-to RHR is a giant cocktail ring (which you would wear on your right hand), made up of a 25-ish carat light-blue single emerald-cut stone. Even though it's a 1950s costume piece likely not worth more than a few dollars, it transforms my entire look. As Elizabeth Taylor once said, "We are all just temporary custodians of beautiful things," and you therefore must do it justice as the confident person that would wear such a beautiful thing. Now, the next time you are having "one of those days," simply pull out the right-hand-ring move, and you'll be set.

Jewelry and Accessories

This brings me to wearing jewelry. It doesn't matter if it's real or costume or a mix of both. Be cautious of wearing too many diamonds outside of religious or marital jewelry during the day, as they can look flashy, which is not a good thing when it comes to being showy about wealth. Major diamond sparklers come out after 6 p.m. During the day, metallic jewelry like silver, platinum, or gold as well as pearls and gemstones are appropriate. After 6 p.m., dazzle away with and bring out the big, glittery pieces. This is even a rule that the Duchess of Cambridge follows.

My grandmother once told me the story of how she went to a black-tie evening event and wore a diamond necklace with a sapphire as big as a blueberry that glittered for days. This necklace, she told me, did not have a real stone in it but looked stunning and made her feel like a million dollars. As she walked into the room, she knew all eyes were on her. As necks craned, and cocktails flowed, eventually the other women came over to say hello (a.k.a., get a closer look). My grandma said she never lied and told them it was real, but she never told them it was not. When someone would comment on how incredible the necklace was, she would simply look back and humbly say, "Why, thank you." The lesson here is that you can wear anything you want that makes you feel amazing. As long as you wear it with confidence, nobody can question it.

Avoid a cluttered look with too much jewelry or too many accessories. I have a "pick-3 rule" which of course has its exceptions, but generally speaking it works for day-to-day dressing. When you get dressed—again, besides marital or religious jewelry—choose up to three pieces of jewelry. For accessories, I recommend choosing one statement piece such as a scarf or tie, for example. Any more than that risks looking cluttered and can distract from an overall put-together appearance.

Organize and Prepare

There are many things to be aware of to help keep a classic and sophisticated look. Another tip is to organize and prepare yourself the night before. I know you may be thinking you don't have the time to do this, but this is simple prioritizing, and your personal presentation should be a priority when you want to get ahead in life. All it actually requires is ten minutes a night before you go to bed. Lay out what you plan to wear (accessories and all) for the next day, and hang it overnight so it doesn't wrinkle. Especially if you're not a morning person, it allows you to have your alert night-self choose your clothes for you so you don't have to think about it the next day. I keep one "emergency" outfit that I can put on at any time that I feel great in. I have three pairs of the same trousers, and three pairs of the same blouse, and I know those are my go-tos when I don't feel like thinking about it. This is what some of my clients who are the most successful and polished people in the world do, which helps them start the day off organized and confident, saving morning brain power to conquer the day. On that note, I thought it may be helpful to have a list of do's and don'ts to guide you in your dressing and personal presentation style:

Do:

Go for tailored, not tight clothing. If you can pinch your clothing and it pings back onto your skin like an elastic, it's too tight. If you squat and feel like you will pop out or tear your trousers, again, it's too tight. Instead, take your clothing to a tailor and have it trimmed to fit you. I go three times per year to a little, family-run tailor in my neighborhood and bring all of my clothes to be tailored at the same time. The goal is that each piece of clothing looks like it was made for you. Choose good quality fabrics that won't pill, bobble, or wrinkle easily. When shopping, aside from silks, try taking a small handful of the fabric you are looking at in your hand. Squeeze it in your fist for two seconds and let go. If it remains a crinkled mess, think twice about buying it. Wrinkled clothing is a sign of untidiness and laziness, and if ironing isn't your thing, try a small, handheld steamer. When I travel, I carry a plug-in one that fits in my carry-on and takes out creases in seconds.

Do:

If you are having a lazy day running errands, follow the 2-of-3 rule. I first heard of this rule from a client of mine and instantly loved it. The idea is that realistically not every day will allow for the time to put yourself together 100 percent, but you still want to look polished and be "on brand" when you go out in public. Therefore, before you leave the house, make sure you have at least two of the three in check: Hair, Skin, Clothing. So, if you walk out to run errands and you have athleisure on, make sure your hair is nicely combed or styled and your skin is fresh and taken care of. This could mean putting on makeup or even just moisturizer. If you are a man and you walk out of the house and your hair is a bit wild, make sure your outfit is slick and your skin looks great, which includes shaving your face or trimming your beard. If your skin or makeup is on point, you can slack a little on either the outfit or hair. I love this rule and use it myself on the days when I'm momming it around town running errands with a toddler attached to my hip.

Do:

Wear brown shoes if you have on a brown belt. Black shoes? Then, yes, black belt. Also remember the darker the suit, traditionally the more formal. To wear a light beige suit in winter would not be as formal as wearing dark grey, blue, or black. Another thing to consider is the material of a suit. In summer you may look perfectly appropriate in a lighter fabric such as linen to accommodate the heat. In winter, however, a linen suit wouldn't cut it for function or fashion reasons. I am absolutely fine with mixing black and navy, even though many think it clashes. I think it looks super chic and modern. At the end of the day, you have to wear what makes you feel great.

Do:

Wear white year-round. One of the oldest and most antiquated fashion "rules" is that you should only wear white from Memorial Day until Labor Day, and then avoid it like the plague the rest of the year. This hails from the late 1800s and early 1900s when only the wealthy could afford seasonal clothing such as white linen for summer holidays. Wearing an all-white wardrobe during the summer months indicated which class you are in. It's quite ridiculous if you think about it nowadays, and can even be seen as showy to pull out your all-white wardrobe for these reasons. Even Coco Chanel thought this rule was ridiculous and chose to wear white all year. I wear winter white, summer white, and fall creams whenever my heart desires, and I think you should, too. Only time not to wear white? Unless you are the bride, do not wear white (or off-white, or even that pale, light pink gown that looks white-ish in photos!) to an engagement party, bridal shower, or wedding. It's a major faux-pas, because all attention should be on the bride and/ or groom and by donning white to their wedding celebrations, you're wearing the color designated for the one getting married, hence appearing to take the attention away from the bride and onto yourself.

Do:

Hold your handbag (it's a handbag, not a purse . . . a purse is for change!) like this:

Option 1: YES! The handle of the bag goes in the middle of the forearm, wrist facing up.

Option 2: NO! Holding the strap at the crease of your elbow where your hand crooks down. I call this "the dinosaur" as it looks like Tyrannosaurus Rex.

Option 1: YES! Do not put your clutch in the pit of your arm, but instead hold it in front of you or to your side. The same goes for an iPad, presentation folder, or anything similar.

Option 2: YES!

Option 3: YES!

Don't*:*

I'm not saying to throw out anything with a brand or logo on it. I'm simply saying to proceed with branded items in moderation. Too many or too large logos may be seen as a sign of insecurity. The negative connotation is that when wearing obvious logos, one needs to show the world how much they spent on something or align themselves with a brand when they should focus on being their own brand without showcasing their wealth. Some of my wealthiest clients in the world, who can afford any brand they want, refuse to wear branded clothing. These people, who have unlimited funds, have everything made for them. Think of the royal family; you don't see their dresses and suits or ties with logos written blatantly across them.

Don't:

Wear only trendy clothing. Stick to pieces that would look good five years ago and five years from now. If you haven't worn something in a year, it might be up for election for your donation pile.

Decoding the Dress Code

Oscar Wilde said it best: "You can never be overeducated or over-dressed." When in doubt, always dress more formally. Organized events such as parties or weddings often require a dress code. So, what does it all mean? Here is your cheat sheet to dress codes.

Casual: Relax! Comfortable and informal clothing, yet coordinated appearance.

Business casual: Professional appearance still required. No T-shirts or flip-flops. Ladies, avoid spaghetti strap or strapless options. Instead, try a blouse or top that has some sort of sleeve or thicker strap. The hemline of any dress or skirt should be slightly above the knee at most. To test if your shorts, dress, or skirt is too short, stand with your shoulders rolled back and put your hands to your sides. If your dress/skirt/shorts come above the lowest point of your middle finger, they are likely too short. No bra straps showing, please! Gentlemen should keep to collared shirts whether it be a polo or button-down. Always tuck in your shirt, and use a belt if the trousers you are wearing have belt loops. Wear shorts only if you are off-site or if company culture allows them.

Cocktail/Semi-formal/After 5 p.m.: For ladies, a little black dress, silky jumpsuit, or cocktail dress sparkles. For men, pending the formality of the event and venue, a jacket with pocket square or jacket and tie would be appropriate. If you're not sure if a tie is required, bring one as a backup.

Formal: The length of your dress should match the venue along with the formality of the event. A knee-length dress, tea-length (to your calf muscle) dress, or floor-length dress may be absolutely appropriate depending on the event. If you have a formal wedding in a garden, a knee-length dress may be perfectly fine, but for a formal wedding at The Plaza Hotel, I'd go for a long dress. For gentlemen, I recommend suit, tie (bowtie or regular), and jacket. For an extra wow, add a pocket square.

Black tie/After 6 p.m./Very formal: Floor-length gowns for ladies. For men, I recommend a traditional tuxedo with a black bow tie.

Resort/Island elegant, beach chic, garden party, outdoor day wedding: Think cocktail party (usually during the day) with more casual fabrics: linen shirts and blazers for men, and flowy dresses in florals in bright colors for ladies. Save the more sparkly pieces for after 5 p.m.

Common Dress-Code Questions

Q: How much skin is *too much* skin?

A: I have a rule about showing skin. It's the same that I see practiced in the Palace, and I call it the "pick one" rule. If you have open shoulders, choose a longer hemline. If you have a shorter hemline, cover the shoulders. Too much skin tends to look less polished and leaves nothing to the imagination.

Q: Is it ever okay to show cleavage?

A: A bit of cleavage for me is something only to be seen in more formal occasions when you have an elegant dress that has a beautiful neckline that dips slightly lower than usual. I agree it's extremely important to love your body, but there are ways to accentuate your figure and curves without giving it all away when wearing everyday attire. Avoid cleavage altogether in professional attire, and let people focus on how brilliant your brain is instead.

Q: Is it advised to avoid clothing with slits?

A: If a dress or skirt has a slit, it was likely put there for function to help you walk easier. This means when buying clothes, look for a subtle slit (preferably at the back of a dress or skirt) and only a couple of inches. A slit up the front of a skirt or dress can go wrong pretty fast. On occasion we see an elegant black-tie dress that has a higher than normal-for-function slit, and that would be the only exception to this point.

Q: I love stockings but are they considered old-fashioned?

A: Stockings: tights, pantyhose, whatever you want to call them. I like them when it comes to a formal business (corporate meeting) or conservative social event (entering a religious ceremony in a place of worship).

Q: What are the biggest no-no's that make you look less-than polished?

A: First one would be sun or eye glasses on heads. Either wear them or put them away. Remember, if they are not on your face, they should be in their case! Second, I'd say overstuffed handbags with shoes falling out. Carrying multiple bags at once such as a gym bag, briefcase, and lord knows whatever else is also a no-no. Learn to consolidate your packing and clean out your bags so you only carry what you need. Finally, avoid scuffed, unpolished, or dirty shoes. I think shoes are an easy accessory to make anyone look a little more razzle-dazzle. An old friend's grandfather once said, "Don't skimp on your shoes or your bed, because if you're not in one then you're in the other."

Q: There are so many styles to tie a tie. Which do you recommend?

A: For a classic look, I prefer the Windsor or Half-Windsor tie knot. Classic, elegant, and chic, while perfect for any occasion.

Q: What do you think about beards or other facial hair?

A: I think facial hair can look rather dashing on some men (think Prince Harry on his wedding day!) but the key is that it's got to be perfectly groomed and look intentional. Sporting a five o'clock shadow may not be the best look unless you are on vacation, as it may come across as lazy that you didn't take the time to present yourself.

Meier Method Step 2

ATTRACT

Welcome to step 2 of The Five Step Meier Method! Now that you have learned some of the more outward polishing, we are ready to work on the inside polishing. This next section offers key soft skills that can give you the confidence to attract the people, opportunities, and life that you want. Be warned that reading on may lead to endless social invitations, becoming the life of the party, and having an adoring circle of friends. If you want to learn next level secrets to the law of attraction, this one is for you.

Chapter 4

Charisma
Yes, You Can Learn It!

I'm going to tell you a little story here that I think many people can relate to on both a social and professional level. Claire is the smartest executive at work. She is sincere, hardworking, confident, and polished. She walks into her trendy downtown marketing office five minutes early as per usual, and the receptionist greets her with a polite wave and welcoming smile. Claire sees her colleagues, who all nod and give the routine good morning wave as she passes their desks and returns the gesture. She is liked and well-respected. Claire sits, gets settled, and starts her computer for the day.

Only moments later, Mackenzie walks into the same office and suddenly the whole energy of the room shifts. As Mackenzie passes the same desks Claire had moments ago, people beam with delight to see her. Even though Claire is almost identical to Mackenzie on paper in age, looks, and education, Mackenzie is visibly more well-liked, admired, and respected. Everyone wants Mackenzie on their team, at their dinner party, and on their side, because Mackenzie has the ability to make every single person feel as if they are sparkling when they talk to her. She manages to turn a dull conversation into laughter, and puts a tense moment at ease. She is quite simply . . . contagious. She shines even on a bad day and radiates blinding glitter on a good day.

What makes Mackenzie so different from Claire? Mackenzie is the most charming girl in the room. She has charisma. So, what exactly is charm, otherwise known as charisma? It is literally defined as the quality of giving delight, arousing admiration, and the power of attractiveness through emotion. In a room full of faces, charming people have the ability during conversation to make others feel as though they are the only other person in the room. People are left feeling flattered and important. Charm is the ability to connect deeply with others and make even the most opposite of strangers feel welcome. Charming people are irresistibly engaging, attractive, charismatic, and gracious. Charm is arguably one of the most important qualities both socially and professionally that one person can attain. It makes you unforgettable, admired, and ultimately successful wherever you may go.

You can be the smartest worker in the office, the best dressed person at the ball, and the most fit and well-groomed person at the party, but if you have none of those things and only charm, it will trump all other factors. So, can charisma be learned? Absolutely. Want to learn the secret to it all? Remember this next sentence above all else: Charm is all about evoking positive emotion in someone else. Not just any emotion, but *positive* emotion.

Charisma

I truly believe that charm is your secret weapon both socially and professionally. Below is a formula I created which includes the main components to remember when trying to come across more charming and charismatic. Think of this formula like a recipe in the way that one element without the next is not complete. If initially you can master only a couple, or perhaps none of the below, focus on adding one at a time until you are able to practice all at once when communicating. From the moment you enter a room or situation, start practicing these components.

Meier Method Formula for Charisma

- Maintain a positive attitude
- Create the best first impression
- Create a likable persona
- Project confidence
- Change negative perceptions
- Overcome fear
- Surround yourself with happy people
- Stand out . . . humbly!

Maintain a Positive Attitude

You probably can't think of a charismatic person who is a downer, can you? Successful, magnetic people don't let others feel negative energy. When you walk into a room, nobody wants to hear that you had a bad day or don't feel good. Even if I'm having a bad day, while I'm not expected to ever be dishonest, I never share this negativity with others I want to connect with. Example: I walk into class after a difficult morning, and when someone asks me how I am, I might reply, "Let's just say this coffee made my morning!" and leave it at that. Always try to find the silver lining in any situation.

Create the Best First Impression

Here is where you can start putting into practice what you already learned so far in this book. In Chapter 3 (page 38) we learned how to make a best first impression. Try making a new first impression every day if you need to. Don't be shy if people you have known for years start commenting on how different you seem. Take it as a compliment and know that the changes you are making are working! If your neighbor "negative Nancy" points out (in a rude way) that you have "changed," don't be afraid to own it. For example, if Nancy says,

"Why are you dressing different all of a sudden?" your answer might be, "You know, I realized I wanted to step it up a notch so that I felt my best." Boom. How can Nancy possibly argue with that?

Create a Likable Persona

The secret to being likeable is approachability, relatability, and the ability to connect instantly with people. If you can walk into a room and make someone feel good, they are likely to be receptive to you. In summary, this means walking into the room with a smile, showing bright eyes, and positive, open body language. Dressing in a way that makes you appear to have put effort into your appearance to show you wanted to be respectful to yourself and others. Make good eye contact with people. Compliments feel good to hear, so don't be afraid to give them. Be relatable. If you walk into a room and are not relatable mostly through conversation, you won't connect. If you can't find something to talk about that is relatable to others, show genuine curiosity and ask them questions about themselves (nothing too personal at first). The bonus is if you can use humor to communicate. Humor is often just simply making light of a situation in a non-offensive way.

Project Confidence

This is a hard one, I know. That's why I have built an entirely separate "how-to" formula (page 68) to help you gain confidence in any situation.

Change Negative Perceptions

Years ago, in one of my first jobs, my boss told me that I was too shy in meetings and not speaking up when in the presence of clients. The core of the reason was that I wasn't confident in my role and was intimidated by my own clients. I knew my stuff; I just didn't know how to get it out of my head and deliver it. In that moment, I knew I needed to change this negative perception and fast. Therefore, the first step is to write down the negative perceptions you think someone has about you, or even feedback you've been given (professionally or socially). That's the hardest part. Then, it's time to tackle each point, one by one. In my case, I knew I had to start speaking up in meetings with my clients so my boss had confidence that I could handle them. Days before the next weekly meeting, I made a list ahead of every point I wanted to discuss in the meeting and didn't leave the meeting until I addressed each point written down in front of me. I found I had a hard time interjecting into the conversation, so I made myself more authoritative. If you're having issues with achieving authority, see my Meier Method formula to gain authority, also in this chapter (page 82). After that meeting, my boss said in the elevator, "I've never seen that side of you! Well done." My reply was, "Thank you for your feedback after the last weekly meeting. I'm glad you brought it to my attention." I did this to not only acknowledge that these changes were very intentional, but also to show that when someone gives me criticism, I can turn it into constructive criticism. I was able to turn a real negative into a career highlight by being strategic about changing negative perception about myself.

Overcome Fear

This is my favorite point because the faster you can learn to put this into practice, the faster things will start happening for you. Fear in a social sense can be debilitating. Ask yourself this: Who is the most charming person you can think of? It can be a friend, family member, or even a fictional character. Picture this person right now. My guess is that this person is extremely confident, compelling, and outspoken. You know what I bet they are not? Fearful. The thing about charismatic people is that they say what they want, do what they want, and ultimately get what they want. It's the fear of failure that prevents us from doing what we want. Imagine trying to walk through a door that is closed. What would happen? You would walk straight into it until you opened the door to let yourself out. We treat fear as if it were a door, a physical blockade we cannot walk through, but fear is not an actual physical block. You are the only one standing in the way of your success. I live by the famous question, "What would you attempt to do if you knew you could not fail?" If you take fear out of your vocabulary, you'll be amazed at what you can do. Start today.

If you feel fear creeping back in, don't think about it, just do it! I often chant to myself in my head "don't think, just do." The longer you wait and analyze, the more fear will creep in and actions will be harder to do. One example of how I used this is the day I met my husband. I was heartbroken from a breakup and hiding in my dark NYC apartment one September day. Tina, one of my best friends I'd known since college, practically dragged me out of bed, dressed me, and brought me down to the mecca of brunches, a place called Pastis. We drank rosé and talked about all the reasons I was not meant to be with my ex. As we listed the reasons, I gazed over the crowd of beautiful men and women chatting and flirting. While so chic, the entire crowd was dressed in black. "Where is my Palm Beach, pink-shirt guy? Maybe I'm in the wrong city," I said out loud. Tina and I made our second stop of the day to Felix, a fun brunch spot in Soho that glittered with social swans and was known for its European clientele. It wasn't long before I felt a sharp nudge in my side. "Myka, there he is," Tina said while nodding to the door. It was as if the crowds parted and it was at that moment that I saw him. Walking in the door with a group of gorgeous Zoolander-like friends was one man wearing a pastel pink button-down shirt. Sandy blonde hair, high cheek bones, a smile like a dream. (Oh, and cufflinks. *Bingo!*) "The rosé went down a little too easy and I definitely cannot speak to him," I said, watching Tina roll her eyes.

"It's fate. You asked for him and here he is, standing in front of you. Now, go!" She physically pushed me toward him and I began walking straight to him.

"Don't think, just do. Don't think, just do," I repeated to myself. Suddenly I was there, standing in front of him. Our eyes locked and it was too late to turn around now. I blame the rosé, but as I stood there, I literally could not think of anything clever to say except "Hello. I just wanted to come introduce myself, my name is Myka." A total I-carried-a-watermelon moment. Now, you'll have to come see me in person to hear the rest of the details, but that was the moment of no fear that changed my life forever. A few years later I was married to Marco, who wore the same pink shirt to our beach wedding reception. And yes, Tina was my maid of honor, and now the godmother of our daughter Valentina. The moral of the story, however, is that had I been too fearful to approach him, I likely never would have met him. My advice to you? Write down a list of what you want and go get it, like now!

Surround Yourself with Happy People

Sure, it's arguable, but I'm pretty convinced that happy people are the most attractive. Are you happy? If not, only you can change that. Do you surround yourself with happy people? There is a saying that you are a culmination of the six closest people to you. It's an interesting exercise. Make a list of those six people. Are they all energy draining and are you constantly only giving your time to them without any balance or exchange of joy in return? Are they exceptional, positive, supportive, and uplifting? Perhaps there is a mix. It's okay to understand that throughout life our six can change as we grow in different phases of our lives, and we may need to adjust the role these people play. I also think that the happiest and most fulfilled people are often those who are the most grateful and thoughtful. Finally, the most joyful people I know love to make other people happy. My mom, for instance, is the most thoughtful person I know. She picks me up from the airport literally every single time I fly home to Florida, and arrives with my favorite cupcakes from our local bakery. The house is filled with the most glorious smell when I arrive home. She has made my favorite meal, spaghetti with her special homemade Bolognese sauce and hand-rolled meatballs. She does this because she loves the joy it brings me and it makes her happy to make me happy. It's the little things.

Stand Out . . . Humbly!

If you blend in, you may be doing yourself and everyone else a disservice. If you feel fantastic wearing all purple head to toe, you should wear it. If it's not popular to go somewhere or do something that you're passionate about, but you really love it, you should do it. Don't be afraid to stand out from the crowd. I remember when I was interviewing for my first job in London and saw all the women wearing black, tight clothing and tons of makeup. I wanted to fit in so when I got the job I went out and bought all the same clothing and makeup, but on my first day of work I had zero confidence and felt self-conscious because it felt like I was wearing someone else's clothes. I tried hard for one week until I realized I was failing miserably, so I walked in the next Monday head to toe in a bright pink cable-knit cashmere sweater, oversized pearl earrings, and Ralph Lauren knee-high leather boots. That was me and I felt fabulous. I must have heard every American joke in the book that week, but I was able to feel confident again in my own skin, even if nobody else looked like me. And you know what? They respected me for it because I was unapologetically me.

Now, another thing to note about standing out is that if we do something that we are proud of or excited about, while it's of course okay to share it, we must always remember to be humble. If you give a killer presentation at work for instance and afterward people are coming up to you left and right to say how amazing it was, it's easy to say thank you and smile with a cheeky "I know" grin. But you can't. Well, I mean, sure you can, but I wouldn't recommend it. Likeable people are not cocky people, so let's rewind here . . . you give a killer presentation at work and afterward people come up to you to say how amazing it was. My recommended response is to always say thank you and acknowledge their compliments, but the formula is gratitude followed by a piece of humble pie. "Thank you, that's so kind of you. I truly couldn't have done it without my amazing team who helped put it all together." *Or* "Thank you! I really have so much more work to do still, but I truly appreciate your kind words." Essentially, the trick is show gratitude to anyone who says how wonderful a job you did or compliments you in any way, but the accolade should never appear to be one that you personally give yourself. Always be humble. Myka-ism: Humble Henry has hordes of hens . . . and I'm not talking about the bird, either.

Charming person bonus: Always, and I mean *always*, be kind. My dad is one of the sweetest humans on earth and taught me this lesson early on. I remember him telling me to be nice to everyone, smile at everyone, and to the mean ones, "kill them with kindness" as they probably need it most. I also grew up observing another influential couple in my life, my Grandpa and Nana. One day I realized, after witnessing their reactions to an aggressive driver in a drive-thru parking lot, that even when it was someone else at fault, neither would ever say an unkind word about or to someone else. Literally never once. I live by these inspirational people's lessons.

Meier Method to Increasing Confidence

If someone could figure out how to bottle confidence and sell it, they would be a billionaire. Sadly, while that is not possible, if you want to increase confidence in any situation, I created a formula that I use to help give myself a boost when I need it. Here is my secret for you to also use if you ever need it. Just remember, you are enough, you have enough, and you are pretty fantastic as-is.

First, it's important to understand the difference between confidence and self-esteem. Confidence is what we project and what we want others to see, while self-esteem is how we really feel inside. Truly comprehending the difference is important because while confidence can change from day to day or even hour to hour, self-esteem is much deeper rooted and less volatile.

That being said, you can have low self-esteem, but still be able to walk into work every day with great confidence or show confidence on a date. Confidence is attractive. While it's important to know how to show or feel confidence in a situation or scenario, it's important to work on having high self-esteem regularly. Do you find that your self-esteem has always been on the lower side? Remember my saying, "Don't fake it until you make it, practice it until you become it." This works with confidence and self-esteem, too.

Win an Oscar . . . in Confidence

I'm going to teach you a little game called "win an Oscar" that you can play along with me. I started doing this in London with my friends, and now teach my students this, too. Here's how it works. If you are about to walk into a situation that you just don't feel confident going into, you have to pretend that all of a sudden you are on a movie set, and there is a camera on you. Instantly you have to take on a role in whatever scenario you have just been thrown into. Improv acting if you will. You must now act in this scene as the confident character you would see in a movie. The goal is to win a proverbial Oscar for your performance. How can this play out in real life, you might be wondering? I am not the most comfortable public speaker of groups of more than one hundred, so when I have to speak in front of a group of one thousand people or more, I often do this before going out on stage. I never feel at ease before I go on stage, but after learning deep breathing exercises, and practicing over time, I have gotten more used to it. The first time I had to do it, I called my husband ten minutes before I was to go on stage, as I was feeling light-headed and panicked. Without hesitation, he reminded me of my own technique. "Okay, you're there. I know you're in your power suit and I know you're going to do amazing. Now, go win that Oscar!" Suddenly I was able to snap into character, ready to go. All cameras were on and rolling and I had to "act" the part starting that very second. Action! Imagine it almost as your alter ego sets into motion. Come up with a name for that person if you need to. I did. When I need to jump into my alter ego to go win that Oscar, you can bet your bottom dollar that I have now learned to turn it on and off whenever I need to. It just takes practice. I have been able to separate the person who might be struggling with self-esteem for any reason, from the person who can control confidence like a light switch when I need to. After giving birth, I remember not being able to fit into any of my clothes, all my hair falling out, having adult acne on top of it, and feeling like I was in a new body that I didn't understand. I had low self-esteem about my personal appearance and it was during this time that I used the win an Oscar technique often to get myself back to the place I wanted to be. I still had to function and get out socially and

I had to win an Oscar many times over. It's a great Meier Method to snap in and out of any situation.

Your Love List

To gain confidence, some people stand in front of the mirror practicing their "power pose" and practice making direct eye contact in the mirror. This was something I could never do for some reason, and always ended up giggling like a school girl when I tried. If you feel the same, try another Meier Method to feel confident called a "love list." Here's how you do it: On your phone or in a notepad, make a list in a row of all the words you would love to feel, exude, and strive to be. Your love list could be five words or fifty, and is totally up to you. Read your love list in private right before you need to project confidence. For instance, even though I'm not the most comfortable public speaker, I no longer need to call my husband every time I walk on stage; I just read my list. I pull out my phone about ten minutes before I get my microphone attached to my blouse and I will slowly and consciously read each point. It reminds me of who I am, who I want to be, and who I love being. Even if I'm not all those things all the time, they are the things I need to project via my confidence when I walk on stage. For instance, my love list may look like this:

- Powerful
- Inspirational
- Kind
- Witty
- Funny
- Sophisticated
- Charismatic
- Brave
- Oprah
- Graceful
- Motivational
- Confident

Okay, if you read all the way through my list, you might have noticed I included Oprah's name. This is to show you that there are no rules to the love list and you can include anything on it that inspires you, that you want to project, or that you want people to feel or take away from meeting you. You can also include names of people that you want to channel or that you admire. In my case, Oprah is the most confident woman on stage that I can think of. Your love list can change and evolve over time and grow with you. In addition to those ideas on how to feel more confident, by now, you probably know that I'm a formula person. I love to be given formulas to follow, and therefore I love to create them, too. Learn how to project confidence in any situation with this easy to follow formula below:

Meier Method Formula to Confidence

1. Package yourself
2. Voice
3. Build rapport
4. Understand what "sparks" you
5. Organize yourself
6. Emulate
7. Practice!

1. Package Yourself

This refers to how you present yourself, including both your appearance and your posture. Posture as we have learned is crucial body language to show you are confident. Put yourself together so you feel great and look polished. Remember, if you don't like what you're wearing that day or don't feel good in it, it projects into the rest of your day. Everything else in this formula can be on point, but if I believe you are self-conscious about your appearance or personal presentation points we learned about, it shows. Remember, you are a complete package.

2. Voice

You could walk into a room wearing your power suit or gorgeous outfit and killer shoes, dressed to perfection and with perfect posture, but the moment you open your mouth and a less-than-confident voice peeps out, you suddenly lost the confidence of those around you. Stop and think about this one. Visualize the most confident person you can think of. It could be a friend, colleague, or even a fictional character. You don't see them enter a room or a conversation shyly through their voice. They often have a very powerful voice. This doesn't mean a loud voice, but unwavering, solid, with a good pitch, and commanding a presence.

3. Build Rapport

To build rapport is another important part of the confidence formula. Walking into any social situation, if someone is familiar with you and can relate to you, you become more likeable. Building rapport gives your confidence ammunition in the same way that knowledge gives you power. For example, if you already know the person you run into at a social event, try to build a rapport with them. "The last time we saw each other, your children were just starting school. How has the year been for them so far?" Simply showing someone that you remember them and your conversation makes them feel important and will instantly encourage them to engage with you. I sometimes take notes on important contacts and save them on my phone so that the next time I plan to see them, I can pull it out and remind myself before I speak with them again. It might be as simple a note as "Bron – met at Shane's house – wife named Christine, daughter Erica. Going to Zurich for Xmas." By making these notes, putting in this effort, and ultimately building rapport, I am more confident going into the social situation or conversation, and it shows.

4. Understand What "Sparks" You

This essentially asks the question, "What is it that makes you *not* feel confident?" If something sparks you, it challenges you. First, identify the thing or list of things that sparks you. Then, make a list. This is often a hard exercise to do because it forces you to face insecurities that maybe you'd rather not admit. Once you have this list of what is making you feel not confident, you're not done there. Next, you need to make a plan of how to address each point. Third, you have to do something about it and put your plan into action. Just to make a list of what sparks you isn't going to do much except frustrate you. Once you have an action plan for overcoming each point, you have a roadmap on what you need to do to change these things. Finally, remember "don't think, just do," meaning get started today. Now! That's the hardest part, but before you know it, your list of what sparks you will grow smaller and smaller.

5. Organize Yourself

If you feel scattered and disorganized, it's likely to trickle into your confidence in many ways. If you are prepared, you appear poised. If you are poised, you appear in control. If you are in control, you appear confident. This point may mean different things to different people. For instance, it may be that you are not a "morning person" and constantly sleep through your alarm so you end up running out of the house late and looking disheveled. If that's you, I would take this point and use it to plan ahead the night before and organize myself by setting three timers, two alarm clocks spaced five minutes apart, and a third timer on the coffee machine to automatically turn on in the morning. Another example is that maybe you have been given the honor of best man at a wedding and are asked to give a speech. The only issue is that you're not the best public speaker. In this case, I'd ask you to plan ahead and organize your thoughts by writing them down on index cards and practicing your speech until you know it and don't need to read from your notes any longer. Once you know that speech, you will be confident to give it.

6. Emulate

Watch and emulate people who have confidence. Again, think of the most confident people you know or can visualize. How do they carry themselves, interact with others, speak, dress, or present themselves? By studying people who do things well, you can learn from them.

7. Practice!

This is my favorite point because it's the practical homework of the formula where you have to practice projecting confidence. Like social training wheels; you are getting ready to take them off, but before you do, you need to test out your skills first. Practice at home and when nobody is looking, practice in all areas so that it starts feeling second nature to you. If you only use these techniques when you need them, you likely won't feel or appear confident, but if you have been practicing all the time, you won't feel a bit of difference when you walk into that party, and your confidence will shine. Using the "new you" which is the new *confident* you, try going to a place you have never been before to test out your new techniques. This could mean walking into a coffee shop downtown or a clothing shop. Walk in and using your new appearance, new voice, new demeanor, and new posture, present the new full-package-you to a stranger. By acting differently, only you know that this may feel odd or awkward, so you can rest easy that nobody is judging your sudden changes.

Chapter 5

How to Be Likable

Becoming the Most Coveted Party Guest

Who doesn't want to be liked? Who doesn't dream of being the most coveted party guest? May I introduce you to a Meier Method called ADBA. Another Myka-ism, this is an acronym for Approachable, Drink, Brave, Around. I will teach you what these steps actually mean so that right before you walk into a room you can think this acronym to yourself, follow, and repeat.

ADBA

A is for approachable. Synonyms for approachable are reachable and attainable, and making yourself appear this way is something you must master for successful networking, especially when in groups. Let's go back to the basics here. Phone away, electronic devices away, eyes up, shoulders back. Oh, and the other thing? Remember to smile to be seen as friendly and approachable. We learn this when we are small children trying to make friends, but somewhere along the way, we stopped practicing this most important and simplest action. Often when you walk into a room, all eyes are on you, or maybe perhaps the opposite. Either way, especially when you are alone, this can be uncomfortable. These days it's almost second nature that when we are uncomfortable we reach for our phones to make it look like we are busy or speaking to someone, but by looking down at them we become instantly unapproachable. Because people think you are busy or uninterested in socializing, you may be missing out on amazing introductions or connections. The next time you enter a new environment, try putting your phone on silent and out of sight in your bag or pocket. By practicing good posture (page 24), your body language is saying you are happy to be there.

D is for drink. Once you walk into a room with your personal presentation on point, the next step is to go get a drink. The only exception would be if you saw the host right when you came in and you would of course stop to say hello and thank them for inviting you. If the host was not within immediate eyesight, or there is not a specific host, march yourself straight up to the bar or drink area. Now, when I say get a drink, I must be clear this does not have to be an alcoholic beverage. In fact, it has nothing to do with alcohol. The part that is important however is that you are holding a beverage. People just walking around an event twiddling their thumbs or standing alone in the corner eating are not approachable. The moment you hold a drink, you look like you are there to stay and mingle. All of this being said, if you are not drinking alcohol at a cocktail party, I recommend getting a drink that is ambiguous such as soda water with a lime wedge. Let people assume the content is what they want it to be.

B is for bravery and the hardest part. Now that you look like someone people would want to mingle with, you can't rely on them approaching you first. My technique is to always arrive on the earlier side, because I believe the best networking happens before people pair off into little groups. When you do, if possible, find at least one other person standing by themselves to pair with. It's much easier to have a partner in crime to network with than by yourself. The best place to meet someone? The bar. That's right, it's usually the first place people head to, often leaving their groups to stand in line, giving you the perfect opportunity to start conversation or introduce yourself. I find it easiest to start conversation at the bar, too. "Oh, that cocktail looks heavenly. What is that?" (Why not the food area? Because people are hungry and don't want to chat with strangers while they are jabbing prawn cocktail into their mouths.)

Now, this is where the bravery part comes into play. You are likely going to be the person to have to start conversation, and if this feels unnatural to you, just remember you are not alone and that everyone is in this room for the same reason: to socialize! I'm also willing to guess that everyone shares many of the same insecurities as you, and if nobody introduces themselves, then nobody wins. Be brave, take a deep breath, and remember our mantra: don't think, just do! I find that if I want to talk or introduce myself to someone, I have about a four-second window to do it. I call this the four-second rule. After that amount of time, I start to think too much and analyze all the reasons why I shouldn't, and then I don't. I also think if someone notices you looking at them for more than a few seconds it can become awkward and they will pick up on your hesitation. Hesitation is a sign of lack of confidence in a situation, and like a wolf, the social butterflies will sniff you out in no time! So, the next time you want to speak to someone, don't wait. Just start moving your legs in the direction you want to go and suddenly you will be there standing in front of that person. If you're with a friend who is hesitating to introduce themselves to someone, after reading this book, all you'll have to say to them is "four-second rule" and off they'll go. Works like a charm.

A stands for around. This refers to movement around a room. I have found that people are social creatures of habit. They come into a room or event and find the place they are most comfortable and stay there for most of the night. Think about it, in the social jungle there are those foodies who stand at the food line or near the doors where the caterers come in and out, the people on the lounge sofas, those who stay near the bar, and then the ones standing at high top tables or in a stagnant position somewhere in the room. Therefore, if you are the person moving around, like the little ticking hand of a clock, you will likely meet way more people. I always say "right and around" meaning not to zig-zag through the crowd, but to slowly move around the room meeting people. Maybe some conversations will last a few moments or some much more, but regardless, around the room is the way to meet the most people. Tick-tock you go.

Left-Eye Likable

One of the greatest body language secrets actually has to do with your left eye. Believe it or not, to come across likable, you want to look into the other person's left eye. When you want to come across more authoritative, look into the person's right eye. This technique is mainly due to body language. When standing face to face, shoulder to shoulder with someone else and looking into the other person's left eye, your left shoulder also comes forward, which often happens naturally. By doing this, you are breaking posture and leaning into the other person, which shows compassion and connectivity. When you look into the right eye, what tends to happen is the squaring of shoulders, taking on a more authoritative stance. So, the next time you are at a party or social event and want to come across instantly more likable, remember the alliteration: lean in and left-eye-likable.

Meier Method Step 3

EMPOWER

Welcome to step 3 of The Five Step Meier Method! After learning how to attract people in the last step, this next is about powerful connecting. Ever wish you were brave enough to walk up to just about anyone? The business contact, the love interest, the potential friend that you just stood from afar and thought about approaching but wouldn't dare? We've all been there, but now you're going to learn how to actually make it happen. This next step will help give you a powerful presence and teach you what makes a person influential.

Chapter 6

Powerful Presence

I truly believe that you can be polished and have beautiful manners, but there may still be something missing when it comes to engaging and attracting others. It's a level of wow factor that some people have when interacting. What makes someone appear emotionally strong, secure, and captivating, especially when communicating with others? It's that they have a powerful presence. Especially in an environment with multiple big personalities, having a strong presence earns respect. People who earn respect also earn leadership, and with leadership comes power. Have you ever come across someone in a high position of power that lacks authority? My guess is no. To have authority simply means that you are in a position of influence, and who wouldn't want that? Socially, everyone can think of the person who, when they walk through the door of the party, everyone notices they have arrived. I have had the great honor of working and socializing with some of the most influential people who carry a powerful presence, and after years of analyzing and speaking with them, I started to see patterns. I was able to create a formula that I personally started following and saw instant change in the way I came across to people and the way I was treated by people. May I therefore introduce you to the Meier Method formula which will help you increase your authority in any situation, but also help you build an overall powerful presence.

Meier Method Formula to Increasing Authority

1. Find your voice
2. Control your body language
3. Speak up
4. Make decisions
5. Be confident
6. Get rid of fear

Find Your Voice

The number one thing allowing someone to be viewed as a figure of authority is their voice. It's human nature that we use voice to detect character from another person. It's one of our most used senses when communicating with other people. Think of the president of your social club or the captain of your sports team. Chances are, this person has a powerful voice that commands attention. Remember, powerful voice does not mean loud. It means unwavering, strong, and firm. You can certainly be assured that when I walk into a room of two hundred people there to learn etiquette from me that I have to instantly captivate an audience if I want them to pay attention, and I do this mostly through my voice. There are many ways to work on your voice, from free online tutorials, to public speaking clubs, books, and more.

Control Your Body Language

Once you have your authoritative voice down, it's time to make sure your body language shows everyone that you are in charge, or at least could be if you wanted! Remember that body language is communicating nonverbally. People who are in charge communicate it with their bodies. I will go so far as to say that it's a primitive gesture of power and authority. If your back is curved and you are slouching or walking with your shoulders forward, what you're actually doing is making yourself smaller, shrinking yourself down. In the animal kingdom, when many animals (think birds, baboons, bears, and elephants) want to win a fight or are competing for a mate, they puff out their chests, throw out their ears, and stand tall to make themselves look larger. You would never see an animal wanting to show authority or power suddenly shrink themselves by curving their spines, putting their chins down, looking down at the floor, or allowing their shoulders to roll forward. If you want to show power and increase your authority, you need to command it through your body.

Speak Up

Next, you must learn to be a strong verbal communicator, too. Talk more and have more to say . . . but only when relevant or valuable. To talk just to hear yourself speak is useless. Instead, I want to hear you speak up, but in a way that adds value or context. Another way to increase authority in conversation is to use examples; reference a firsthand story or give a statistic or case study that is factual. Facts are hard to argue with.

Make Decisions

People in positions of authority make decisions. I often see people who will just agree with others in the group, but those who are leaders will often say things like, "I think we should . . . " instead of "I agree that . . . " Don't follow a lead—start the lead. Make a decision and put yourself out there. Don't be afraid of people not agreeing with you. You are brilliant and you have excellent ideas and input.

Be Confident

Remember, confidence is what we project, not often how we actually feel. Be confident. Go back to the Meier Method of Confidence (page 68) if you need to until you have it mastered. Showing confidence is an art form, and it *can* be learned, I promise.

Get Rid of Fear

Last, but equally important is to get rid of fear. A reemerging theme of this book! We spoke about fear in Chapter 4 (page 59) but I can't stress it enough. From this day forward, erase fear from your head and vocabulary. People in positions of authority are not fearful people.

Sophisticated Verbiage

Your voice is arguably the most important part of the Meier Method Formula to Increasing Authority, and I'd therefore like to draw attention to one particular aspect of your voice that is especially important to achieving a powerful presence. I call this sophisticated verbiage. Let's start by asking a simple question: Why is it that generally speaking, people think the British sound so sophisticated? It's not that they have any educational advantages over any other English-speaking country, but they do have a little secret I'm going to share with you. The British enunciate and articulate *everything*, including every consonant, many vowels, and they are very particular about how they do this. Let's take the word "most" or "mostly." In American English if you were to say out loud the sentence, "I think it's mostly okay," the majority would pronounce the word "moss-lee," but in British English, you would pronounce that same word "most-lee." Does this mean you should take on a British accent if you're not from England? Absolutely not. Instead, keep the accent or pronunciation of the English you grew up with, and then start adding in the enunciation and articulation part. It will instantly transform your voice. It will take a conscious effort to do this, but start practicing by pulling words out of every sentence to try it with. Even reading lines out loud from your favorite magazine or newspaper is great practice.

Your next challenge is to create a sophisticated verbiage list to interject into your day-to-day vocabulary. I will share some examples with you. Substitute words like "quite" in place of "very," or "lovely" instead of "nice," or "gorgeous" to describe a meal or experience rather than appearance. Make a list of words you love and that you want to start using and then do it! Instead of saying, "It was very hot out today," you might choose to say, "It was quite hot today." With this Meier Method, what you are actually doing here is creating what I call a "communication pause" in the other person who you are speaking with. A communication pause simply means that instead of being able to predict what another person is about to say, by suddenly throwing in an unexpected word from your sophisticated verbiage list, you cause the other person to have to pause and comprehend what you just said. It keeps the person you are speaking to engaged, on their toes, and interested in your chat. Do your homework and think of your list, and start using it today along with your new voice.

If people you have known for ages comment in a negative way about you sounding different, don't let them make you feel insecure about it. Instead, say something back like, "Yes, I'm so glad you noticed. I realized I have been mumbling and have made a new conscious effort to fix it." You will quickly put them back in their place (in the nicest of ways, of course), and it will be hard for them to say something negative about that! Remember to embrace these "new you" changes, and don't let anyone knock your confidence in the process. Eleanor Roosevelt said it best: "No one can make you feel inferior without your consent." Remember, I will say this until I'm blue in the face: don't fake it until you make it, practice it until you become it! It will take practice and before you know it, that will just be your voice and no longer your "new" voice.

Also, no swearing please. The connotation of swearing is that you don't have the education or mental dictionary to eloquently communicate frustration and therefore need to use the first curse word that pops in your head to describe your feelings. It's also incredibly jarring to hear and should never be done by ladies or gentlemen.

Chapter 7

Social Swan
Network Like a Pro

Meier Method of Networking

Want to become the social swan you know is inside you somewhere and be able to connect to everyone in the room? May I please introduce the Meier Method of Networking. By following this method, you can make and keep conversation with just about anyone. The Meier Method of networking's formula to remember is the TASK acronym which teaches you to **T**arget, **A**pproach, **S**tart, and **K**eep conversation.

Target

I can't tell you the number of times I have walked into a room without a plus one and not known a single soul when I enter. The immediate goal? To *look* approachable, to *spot* those most approachable people, and to know *how* to approach them. When selecting a group that you want to break into, you want to target an open group, rather than a closed group. This essentially means that if everyone's shoulders are together in a circle and eye contact is locked within the circle, it's not the best group to approach. Sometimes even two people speaking is still considered a closed group if their body language and eye contact show you they are not open to a new person entering, again shoulders facing directly toward one another and eyes locked. If two people are speaking but their shoulders are angled out to the crowd, that means they are likely open to socializing with others. If a group is in a loose circle, with some bodies facing one way, some shoulders or hips facing the other, that's a good sign the group will be opening in some way in the near future. The key with a closed group is to wait for the time when it becomes an open group before approaching.

Wolf Pack Socializing

So, who should you actually walk up to in a group? After years of analyzing this scenario and through personal experience, I want to introduce you to a strategy I call Wolf Pack Socializing (WPS). Another Myka-ism code word for you to add to the networking tool belt, this strategy will help take the anxiety out of networking. Use WPS to your advantage by carefully planning who to approach first and why.

The alpha: This is the pack leader, and there is always one. This is the person who makes decisions, introductions, has the confidence to let new people in, and will make conversation. This person is usually the "peacock" of the group, noticed first for varying reasons. If that's not enough to identify the alpha personality, look at the group's toes when in a circle chatting. They tend to all be facing the same direction, pointing toward the dominant alpha, who is likely telling a story or confirming one.

The beta: Follows the pack leader, agrees with the pack leader, may even look like the pack leader. Don't be fooled, this is not the decision maker of the group. They are submissive to the alpha and will take on whatever decision to accept (or not!) new personalities that the alpha sees fit.

The fetcher: This is the nice wolf. The most welcoming of the pack and easy to approach. They don't usually approach you, but are open to being approached. Their confidence is shaky and so a nice compliment upon approaching will be well regarded and will open conversation. In human-speak, this is also the first personality likely to leave the group in order to volunteer to get drinks for someone or accompany another member of the pack to get food or to go socialize. This personality is chatty, easy to talk to, wants to be liked, but seeks approval from more dominant wolves.

The protector: This wolf is the negative nay-sayer. The one who likes the group as-is, trusts nobody, and goes for the throat. Proceed with caution.

The neutral: Easygoing, respected by the pack, and non-confrontational, this personality has an opinion, is confident to make their own decisions, and just wants everyone to get along. They are not hunting at the back of the pack, nor the front, but somewhere enjoying themselves peacefully in the middle. This personality tends to be a good conversationalist, mostly because they will ask questions to get to know you, and decide fairly what they think for themselves.

Approach

You now know who you want to speak with, but how you approach them is just as important. At a typical social event, you can start by being brave and simply walking up and introducing yourself. *Gasp!* I know. I do this all the time, and because most people don't, they will usually be pleasantly surprised by your style and admire it. I will often walk up to someone and say, "Hello, I'm Myka. I don't know anyone here so wanted to come say hello and introduce myself." People will likely be impressed by your candor and take you under their wing. You may be thinking that sounds like something you would never do, but that's what this book is about, teaching you techniques that will get you out of your comfort zone. Remember, people are attracted to confident people, who are often brave people.

A few years ago I used ADBA at a cocktail party and before I knew it was standing in a circle of five new potential friends chatting away. I then noticed one woman standing by herself at a high-top table with her drink. My compassion immediately kicked in and I excused myself and walked up to introduce myself to her. She was totally taken aback and said she was so glad I came because she didn't know a single person. I immediately put her at ease, telling her I didn't know anyone before tonight either and invited her over to the group I was in and introduced her. At the end of the evening, she thanked me again and said she'd like to keep in touch. She pulled out her business card, as I did mine, and we exchanged contact information. As I glanced down at her card, it said she was the global brand manager of the company I had been trying to reach professionally for months. After that surprise meeting, you guessed it, her company became my next client. This simply shows that networking works both ways, and you are an etiquette legend in my book if you bring other people into the group by introducing yourself to those by themselves.

Sometimes even if you get the guts to approach a group of people, they are not friendly. If this is the case, I want you to hear me in your head saying "brush it off" and "next." Shake off any unpleasant feelings it gave you and move on. I'll be honest in saying it has happened to me a number of times, too. I still went on to meet great new people the same night by not dwelling on why they were not nice or welcoming. It's their issue, not yours, and you wouldn't want to socialize with people like that anyway, right? Only surround yourself with good people, and anyone starting off like that probably isn't your cup of tea.

Start Conversation

Can't think of how to start conversation? You're not alone. This is often one of the biggest challenges people face, and a constant topic in my courses. Someone who is a natural conversationalist is usually inquisitive. They show genuine interest in the person they are speaking with through thoughtful questions and engagement. This in turn makes the other person feel important. A bad conversationalist only talks about themselves and does not ask questions. The best questions are typically open-ended, meaning the other person cannot simply answer with one word like "good," "yes," or "no." That being said, it's not always easy to do, so if you can't think of an open-ended question off the top of your head, make sure your topics are interesting and have conversation legs, meaning the topic could lead to other great questions.

I have a little conversation starter trick for you. I call it the "back pocket three," which means that before you go to any social event, think of three relevant conversation topics ahead of time that you can pull out of your back pocket when you need to. These topics should be things you are knowledgeable about, current events, non-sensitive newsworthy topics, or general topics of interest to the group you are in. If you find conversation topics hard to think of, do the work ahead of time. Examples of my back pocket three may be:

1. "I'm not sure if you heard, but the symphony is giving an open-air concert this weekend. When is the last time you went to the symphony? (This is a local current event.)
2. "I just joined the ski club of New York. Are you into any sports?" (Regardless of their answer which could simply be a one-word reply, it's something I am into and knowledgeable about and can talk about in an engaging way.)

3. You may have heard about the vote this coming week that would close the local beach for six months. What are your thoughts on this? (This is a newsworthy topic.).

Again, these are all conversation topics that I can pre-plan so that if there is that awkward silence in conversation, I can whip them out of my back pocket. Here are a few additional open-ended conversation topics by category that are generally safe:

Opening conversation starters: "Where did you go over the weekend?" or "What will you get up to this weekend?"

General get to know you: "What's your favorite way to spend any extra time you have?"

You have mutual friends: "How do you know everyone here?"

You live in the same city: "What's your favorite go-to restaurant?" or "What's the best new spot you've discovered lately?"

You're new in town: "I just moved here/I'm new to the office. What are the places I should check out?"

If you're feeling adventurous: "If you weren't living here, what other city would you want to move to?"

Boring conversation that needs life: "I'm planning my next holiday and need inspiration. If you could choose one place on earth you have not been to yet, where would it be and why?"

Random Secret Weapon: The two A's: Art or Architecture. Talk about the architecture in the room or building you are in, a piece of artwork in the room, your surroundings, or the view. A piece of abstract art in the room is a great conversation starter.

Be cautious when talking about the weather, as I always feel it's a dead-end topic. Yes, we all have it in common, but I call it "doorman chat" that really goes nowhere interesting.

No-No Topics

We all know there are conversation topics we should avoid when talking to people we don't know well. These are all essentially topics that could go south and fast. Generally speaking, they could offend someone, cause a negative response, or may hit a sensitive spot that makes someone uncomfortable. You never want to bring up any topic that could in effect cause the other person to feel discomfort. I call these my top nine, or my "no-no nine" conversation don'ts. Some are more obvious than others, but many are common sense not to bring up.

No-No-Nine:

1. **Politics:** You can never assume someone's political views and therefore by bringing up politics you may get in a heated debate . . . and fast!

2. **Religion:** Often a sacred and private topic to many. To comment on a specific religion may be offensive, personal, or hurtful to another person.

3. **Money:** This topic is sure to make most people uncomfortable. Bragging about something you have, asking how much something costs, or even where someone bought something is bad etiquette because it forces them to essentially reveal how much they spent on it. In addition to money, be careful when using the word "cheap." I remember the week I turned twenty-one I went into a wine store to pick up some wine for a party I was hosting.

I asked the store clerk for a suggestion and he showed me a bottle he highly recommended which was actually under my budget. "Wow, that's so cheap!" I exclaimed. I could instantly see his face change and he snatched the bottle out of my hands and put it back on the shelf. "I have no cheap wine here, my dear. I only have *inexpensive* bottles." What I quickly realized is that the word cheap refers to quality, so if you are using it, be cautious when, how, and to whom. That being said, I still to this day try not to give my opinion about something being inexpensive or expensive because maybe inexpensive to me is expensive to someone else. We must always be conscious of how our words may affect other people's feelings.

4. **Sex:** Keep it private. Even using descriptive words like "sexy" make people squirm.

5. **Vices:** To excuse yourself from a party for a cigarette, announce to the office you had too much champagne last night, or to state any vice whatsoever is inappropriate chatter. Someone might not like smoking or think negatively of drinking. By announcing this to the other person, you may automatically cut off their interest in further liaising.

6. **General illness:** To announce you just had the flu over the weekend but you're much better now is a great way to clear the room. Nobody wants to hear about your sinus infection, odd spot on your back, or your cold.

7. **Diet:** Never announce you are on a diet. Sitting across the restaurant table from my dining companions who all announce they are on a diet, may make me, who just ordered the spaghetti Bolognese, feel bad about what I ordered. If you have dietary restrictions, these should be told only to your server at a restaurant, or announced to your host in plenty of time ahead of the dinner party at a private home.

8. **Gossip:** Never, ever, ever gossip. When you're young you learn that if you can't say anything nice then don't say anything at all. I couldn't love that advice any more for adults, too. Not only is it just not nice, but it makes you look bad to talk about someone else. Whenever I hear someone gossiping about someone, I always think that if they'll do it to them, they may do it to me, too. I also think it's a sign of insecurity to be the person gossiping about others to make yourself feel or look better. Just don't do it. It's so unkind and horrible etiquette.

9. **Family specifics:** While it is okay to ask, "So, tell me about your family," and let the person determine how they'd like to reply, it is not okay to ask specifics like, "So, are you married?" or "Do you have kids?" You may get an uncomfortable response like, "I'm actually going through a divorce," or make someone uneasy by asking questions that are too personal.

Bonus: The number one question *not* to ask in a social forum upon initially meeting someone: "So, what do you do?" *Eek*! I know, I know. You probably ask this every time you go out, or at least get asked this question as a first opening conversation starter. The reason I don't recommend this is because it can come off as opportunistic. It's almost like "How can you help me?" or, more blatantly, "How much do you earn?" People who are fantastic conversationalists are way more creative than this. That being said, if someone asks you, it's fine in return to say, "And how about yourself?"

Compliments

Be careful not to compliment marital or religious jewelry. It may draw attention to wealth or religion, which are both sensitive topics to bring up. The main exception here is if there is a newly engaged or married couple, it is common to "see" the ring. Never ask someone how many carats a stone, such as a diamond, is. It can make people very uncomfortable to have to respond. Never compliment someone on a possession and then ask where it was from, as it forces them to essentially say how much they spent on it. If you compliment someone's sweater, for instance, and they outwardly tell you where it's from, that was their choice. Compliment someone when you first see them, and don't wait until twenty minutes into the conversation, as then it doesn't come off as genuine, but more conversation filler. If someone compliments you, it's correct etiquette to say thank you. My go-to is "Thank you, that's so kind." Too often we try to deflect compliments paid to us when we should really be accepting of them and show gratitude for the person's thoughtfulness.

Keep Conversation

Now that you have bravely broken into conversation, you must keep it going. I actually think starting conversation is much easier than continuing it. After years of being in difficult social situations in which I felt that I had little to nothing in common with someone, or got nervous and froze, I had to figure out how to seamlessly converse with anyone about anything. The biggest secret to good conversationalists is that they ask questions, listen, and stay engaged. That's it. Now, to help you one step further, there is actually a strategy you can use to ensure brilliant conversation no matter who you are talking to or even what they are talking about. Let me introduce you to the Meier Method, W-W-H-C. This one is a favorite trick that I use all the time, because you could talk to a wall with this technique and still come out looking like the ultimate conversationalist. Here's how you do it:

To start, we know you must ask one open-ended question after introducing yourself to start the ball rolling. This could be as easy as "So, how do you know (insert host's name)?" Then, it doesn't really matter what they say in their response, but the key is to start W-W-H-C, which stands for What, Why, How, Compliment. This means that after the person answers your initial open-ended question, the next thing coming out of your mouth should be a question that starts with **what**. Once the person answers that question, the next question you ask them should start with **why**. Last, ask the person a question that ends with **how** and give the person a **compliment** so it doesn't sound like you are drilling them with questions. Then, repeat the W-W-H-C process and start your next question again with what. Now the moment you think you're getting clever and you add in a "where," for instance, they could just answer with one word and the conversation stops.

By using this method to good conversation, you are continuing to ask open-ended questions. Truly, it doesn't matter what their responses to each question are, because you are forcing them to answer in more than just a one- or two-word response. You, of course, must listen to all of their responses every time you ask a question in order to make your questions work. Now, hopefully this person also asks questions back, but in the hardest cases when someone doesn't, this is almost a foolproof method to keep conversation going.

Let's see this play out in a mock conversation. We'll make the scenario a social cocktail party of an acquaintance named Dara. After Person A's initial introduction, then their open-ended question, watch how it plays out:

Person A: "So how do you know Dara?"

Person B: "Well, Dara and I went to law school together at Yale."

Person A: "Oh wow, so WHAT was Dara like in law school?"

Person B: "She was a lot of fun but a serious student, too. She was head of the debate team but always had time to throw a good party. Not much has changed!"

Person A: "That's great. So, WHY did you decide after college to move to New York?"

Person B: "Well, it was an easy decision because many of the best law firms are based here."

Person A: "I see. So, HOW did you choose the firm you are at?"

Person B: "I went into corporate law, and interviewed for a bit and settled with XYZ firm because I felt it had the strongest team."

Person A: "That's so impressive that you ended up there (**compliment!**). So, WHAT neighborhood did you choose when you moved to NYC?"

Common Networking Conundrums

I get endless questions every year in my courses about networking and conversation. As I often hear the same questions, I decided to include them below.

Q: Any tips on following up with someone you met when you reach out?

A: When I follow up with someone, I always reference something specific we were speaking about. People have so many conversations over a night and may need a reminder. I also recommend suggesting a next step in that same follow-up if you want to keep the connection going.

Q: What should you do if you're out at a social networking event and you have someone following you around that you don't want to continue chatting with?

A: Ahh yes, I call this "shadow networking." If there is someone else walking around with you or that you can't seem to end the conversation with, take it as a compliment that they felt a connection with you. That being said, if you didn't sign up for a plus one and now have one following you around at a networking event or social party, the best thing you can do is make what I call a "definitive ending" to the conversation. If you have a shadow networker, if you say, "Okay, I'm going to head to the bar now," or "Please excuse me, I need to go to the restroom," the likelihood that the other person says to you "That sounds great, me too!" is high. That's why you must give a firm and definitive ending to the connection. Try something like "While it was nice to meet you, you must excuse me, as I need to go find my friend. I'm sure we will see each other at the next event soon," or something along those lines. What I did there was give a firm stop on the conversation, then gave a reason, and then commented on the next time we would see one another. Now, remember never to burn a bridge or be rude to someone. You never want to hurt another person's feelings, and you certainly don't know who that person knows or where you will meet them again.

Q: What if I forget someone's name?

A: If you meet someone at an event and at the same event you forget their name, it's perfectly appropriate to ask them again. The biggest key to remember is to say, "Please excuse me, can you remind me of your name?" and not say, "Please excuse me, I have forgotten your name," as by saying you *forgot* them may make them feel unimportant. When I walk into a room and am unsure if I have met everyone in the room or not, I will never reintroduce myself but will instead say, "Good evening, it's lovely to see you." Then, when someone comes up and introduces themselves to me, I know I haven't met them before. It's very hard to recover when you introduce yourself to someone and they say, "Yes, we have met before." *Eek*!

Q: Any tips on how to remember a name?

A: Upon an initial meeting with another person, try to say their name as many times as possible (without sounding awkward) to help you remember their name. For example, if I am just introduced to Beverly and Bonnie, I will say, "Hello Beverly, hello Bonnie. It's so wonderful we could all be here for Tom's party. So, Beverly, Bonnie, how do you both know Tom?" That way, in the first ten or so seconds, I have said each of their names twice, in addition to the time I heard them introduce themselves. I find that names are much easier to remember and stick if you say them out loud.

Q: What should someone do when they encounter a close talker?

A: I'm going to teach you a technique I made up that I call "The Tango" move that I teach to people in my social etiquette courses and even to my private celebrity clients. Sometimes when people are angry or really into you, they get too close to you when speaking. If someone is speaking to you and is not being respectful of your space (or perhaps they are simply not self-aware that they are making you uncomfortable), try "The Tango" technique. First, line up your toes when your feet are flat on the ground. Then, plant your left foot and move your right foot back about 1.5 feet. By doing this, you actually create an invisible line that they cannot cross. Unless they come in to do a tango move and put one of their legs in between yours, they will not cross the front of the left toe which has been firmly planted. Fingers can stay intertwined and put them behind your back. Try it; works like a charm every time!

What Time to Show Up and Why

Timing plays an important role with networking. What time to show up to an event is not only good etiquette to know, but also important so that you can maximize socialization opportunity. I think the best time to get to a group social event, like an organized cocktail party or networking gathering, is about twenty minutes after the start time, and "fashionably late" does not apply. This way you aren't literally the first person to arrive, but it's still early on in the evening, and I strongly believe that the best networking happens at the beginning of the event before people have paired off into conversations or groups. Try it! Note that for a meeting or scheduled appointment, I recommend arriving ten minutes early to take the time to prepare.

Meier Method Step 4

THRIVE

Welcome to step 4 of the Meier Method, the part of the process where it's time to thrive! Now that you have learned the foundation to successful social interaction and the secrets to a polished look, it's time to go out in the world and put these skills to work. The most common way that we do this in the Western world is through dining. You can be utterly charming and win everyone over, and then get to the point in the evening where everyone sits to dinner and lose your footing and confidence if you don't know how to navigate dining etiquette. Therefore, we are going to get you right up to speed on all things dining so you have perfect manners in any social situation.

Chapter 8

Intro to Dining

It's my belief that you should learn more formal training so that you can always adjust to less formal environments. This way, if you are in a high-end place or restaurant, you know exactly what to do and how to act. That's why I will be teaching you formal dining etiquette, so that you can always scale down if you wish. May I please introduce you to the Meier Method Pyramid of Western Dining Etiquette.

Meier Method Pyramid of Western Dining Etiquette

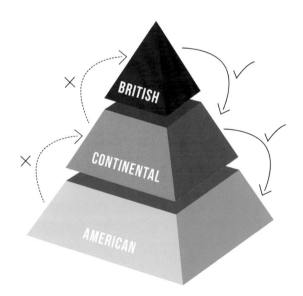

Let's start at the bottom level of the pyramid with the blue section, also labeled American Etiquette. This is the least formal style of etiquette in the Western world. It doesn't mean that it's better or worse than any other style of etiquette, but simply that it's less formal than other parts of the Western world. While I have dual British and American citizenship, and am fiercely proud of both, I love my American roots and how warm and approachable we are as a country. When you are in America, it's excellent manners to practice American etiquette. Remember, to show respect, it's important to always practice the etiquette of the country or culture you are in.

Next up is the orange section, also called Continental Etiquette. Continental etiquette can be used in all of Europe, across the Atlantic Ocean to North America, and all the way through Latin and South America (aside from Great Britain, which is the red section of the pyramid). From the way you hold your cutlery to the way you greet someone, Continental is seen as a very formal style of etiquette. If you are in Europe using it, it's expected and seen as respectful. If you are in North or South America using it, it's seen as formal and quite a sophisticated style. It sets you apart, in a good way.

Finally, the red section at the tippy top of the pyramid is British. It is arguably (mostly by the French) seen as the most formal in the Western world and takes the cake for needing the most practice, especially with dining. While we will not focus on British in this book, if you visit London, for instance, it is recommended to brush up on your British manners in order to show respect and to not stand out in a bad way. Great Britain is the cultural epicenter of stellar etiquette, and one of my favorite countries in the entire world for endless reasons.

What Style Are You Learning?

In this book I will focus on teaching you Continental style of dining because you can use it throughout most of the Western hemisphere (you would switch to British if traveling to the UK) and it is seen as more formal and polished. The one thing to remember about this etiquette pyramid is that you can always travel down but never up, meaning if you practice British Etiquette in America, you will be seen as formal. If you practice American Etiquette in Europe or Great Britain, you will likely raise an eyebrow! That's why I like to teach Continental, because most of your bases are covered in all areas within the Western world. Now, as this book only covers Western etiquette, this means that if you travel to any country outside of it, much of it likely won't fully apply. If you were to go China, for instance, you would switch to Chinese etiquette to show respect to the people and the country.

Formality

Remember that while you will be learning a more formal style of western etiquette, my teaching method and style is very informal so that it's as relatable as possible. When I was learning, I had some wonderful examples of relatability and others that were very intimidating. For me, it was important to make sure that my company Beaumont Etiquette and the Meier Method always make people feel positive, happy, and confident in a judgement-free zone. Think of the lessons in this book like a tool belt. Okay, a really elegant tool belt. It's always best to have all the tools and decide what you need to pull out and when, rather than be in a place where you need a tool and don't have it. Dining etiquette is the next level of education. It sets you apart.

People ask me all the time if I always eat in the formal way, even when I'm on my own. I didn't always, but I do now, and I recommend you do too so it becomes second nature and starts to cement into your daily life. The only exception? Keeping in mind the roots of etiquette, we always want to be relatable to everyone and every situation we find ourselves in, which sometimes means adjusting.

For example, if you are eating formally with your knife and fork at a very casual BBQ and you look around and notice that every other person at the table is eating with their hand, this is when the emotional intelligence alarm kicks in and should signal that you don't want to separate yourself from everyone else. It can come across that you are acting in a pretentious manner. To make everyone around you feel comfortable, I would put down my cutlery and also eat with my fingers. Now, I'm not asking you to "dumb it down" if you know the proper way to eat something but are intentionally not. I am simply advising you to be conscious that we never want to make others feel uncomfortable around us.

The thing I hear most about dining etiquette is that people are terrified of it! Absolutely, utterly terrified to attend a formal meal with more than a course or two, as they are afraid that they won't know which fork or knife to use and how. After reading this chapter, you shouldn't be afraid to host a dinner party or attend one. Knowledge is power, after all.

Dining Basics

1. We practice good table manners to simply show respect to those we are dining with. Another reason why dining etiquette is so important is that it allows you to enjoy conversation, entertain, be social, and enjoy the meal without being self-conscious about what is in front of you.

2. The less noise you make the better and more respectful you are to those around you. This includes everything from voice noise to clinking your cutlery on your plate to your cell phone and other device noises.

3. Confused? Never seen that odd fork before? Not sure how to eat something? Pause and follow the lead of the host. If they are doing something, they surely don't think it's wrong and will not see it as disrespectful if you do as they do. When in Rome!

The Napkin

When you walk into a restaurant, the moment you sit down you should take the napkin and put it on your lap. When you are at a dinner party at a private home, you should wait until the host or hostess puts the napkin in their lap before you follow suit. This is so that we do not rush the host or hostess who may look back at the table and see his or her guests ready and hungry with their napkins on their laps before everyone is seated. In most dining situations, the napkin will be folded and placed on the main dining

plate like the photo here. Note that the napkin should never be folded and put into a cup or wine glass. One of the easiest yet most formal ways to fold a napkin is so that the crease is on the left side of the plate. You can remember this by the 3F's: the Fold Faces the Fork. If you are ever offered a black or dark colored cloth napkin, which typically will be done over fine dining, it is because you are most likely wearing a dark color and the service staff are offering it to you as a considerate gesture so that you do not get white lint on your beautiful threads! Say yes and look fabulous without having to bring a mini lint roller in your handbag or briefcase.

So, how does one elegantly put a napkin on their lap? Unlike a music conductor that whips a prop around with their hands, we want to put a napkin in our lap with as little movement as possible. We take the napkin and gently pull it off the table and bring to our side. We then take the napkin and unfold it totally, then refold it perfectly in half. This is the important part, take the napkin and place it on your lap so that the crease faces toward you. The whole point of this is so that when you clean your mouth, all stains are contained to the inside of the napkin. The goal of the napkin in formal dining is to keep the top, or part that other diners can see, sparkly clean. Therefore, to clean your mouth, you would hold your napkin with two hands and open the edge. It does not matter if it's on the left or right side of the napkin. Then, opening the napkin, bring it up to your mouth. We never lean down to the napkin but instead bring it up so that we maintain perfect posture. Remember when cleaning your mouth, we never "wipe," as you just smear stains in. Instead, we "dab." Remember, Dapper Dan Always Dabs. It's quite fun to say it in your head while doing it, too . . . dab, dab, dab!

Step 1

Step 2

Leaving the Table

If you're going to the restroom, you never tell your dining companions that you are going to the restroom (because who wants to think of what you're doing in there while dining? *Eek*!), and instead we simply say, "Please excuse me." (We do not say, "Pardon me," as that

is terminology reserved for service staff.) When you do need to refer to the bathroom, try calling it the ladies or gentlemen's room, or even the powder room is quite fun if you must ask aloud where other guests can hear. (Fun fact: In the UK, we say lavatory with formal etiquette. Not WC, water closet, or toilet . . . even as much fun as they are to say in a British accent.)

When we leave the table for any reason, we pinch the napkin in the middle and place it in our chairs, then push our chairs in. There is one exception to this rule: if the chair we are sitting on is made of a fabric that can be ruined by anything on our napkins, we would then pinch the napkin in the middle and place it to the left of the place setting, where the forks go.

At the end of the meal, to sig-nify to service staff that we are not coming back and are finished with our meal, we pinch the napkin in the middle of the crease and place the napkin (pinch facing upward) to the left of the plate. We never put our napkins when finished on top of the plate where it could be further soiled, as it creates more work to clean later. You only ever

place the napkin in the "finished" position if you are leaving the table and not coming back.

Where to Place Your Hands at the Table

What about our hands? This is the only part where I recommend not always going Continental, but instead adopting the cultural norm in the country you are dining in. In American and British dining, we keep our hands under the table at all times until we reach above the table to either eat, drink, or gesture. In Continental dining, we would keep our wrists on the table at all times from the moment we sat at the table. In Latin and South America, many countries also have wrists resting on the table.

What about elbows? Is it okay to put them on the table in between courses? No, elbows should never touch the dining table. Ever! It is considered rude throughout all Western culture and should not be done. It also causes us to break posture and look horribly dull.

Holding Glassware

From cocktail parties to dinner parties and everything in between, you may be drinking out of a few types of glasses. The main thing to remember is that if your glass has a stem, you should hold it by the stem. Why? We hold our glasses by the stem and not the bowl of the glass for two reasons. First, it can leave fingerprints, which are unsightly on beautiful glassware. The second and more important reason is because we can heat the liquid in the glass which takes away from the temperature at which it is was meant to be served. This may make perfect sense when thinking of a crisp, chilled white wine, but what about red wine? As many red wines are served at room temperature, is it okay to hold a red wine glass by the bowl? No! Even red wine should be held at the stem because we would never want to heat the wine to more than room temperature, and certainly not to body temperature of 98.6 °F (see more about wine temperatures in Chapter 10 on page 145). So how do we hold a glass with a stem correctly? You want to hold it with a minimum of three fingers: your index, thumb, and middle fingers. It is up to you if you would like to add a fourth or fifth finger to support the stem, as this is sometimes needed with a

heavier glass. I find that the lower to the stem you hold, the more sophisticated a look it becomes.

If you have a glass that does not have a stem, simply keep your fingers together and hold at the bottom of the glass. The less you heat the wine by wrapping your hand around the glass, the better.

When holding a glass of juice or water, commonly served in what we call a highball glass, we keep our fingers all together and at the bottom of the glass so we do not get fingerprints all over the glass. What we want to avoid is what I affectionately like to call "the monster grab," which is where all of your fingers are separated and grasping a glass like I imagine a character from *Where the Wild Things Are* would. When pour-

ing, remember that the "belly" of the glass is the widest point on the glass. In most instances, wine is poured below the belly of the glass.

Water or other beverages such as orange juice that are served in a glass with a stem, however, are served above the belly of the glass.

Holding Cutlery

Now, you can show up to your dinner party looking like a million bucks, but if you don't know the basics of dining etiquette, that's what all the focus will be on. Instead of the attention being on your stunning blouse or gorgeous new slacks, "pretty face, wrong fork" is all they'll be thinking. Not only do you need to learn how to identify the different types of forks and where they are located on the table, but also how to use them. If there is one thing you can do to instantly make yourself look polished at the dining table, it's holding your cutlery correctly.

Index, Wrap, and Twist

No matter if you are left- or right-handed, the fork always stays in the left hand and the knife in the right hand. I'm going to teach you an easy and foolproof method to hold your cutlery correctly in the Continental way each and every time. It's called the IWT: Index, Wrap, and Twist.

Let's begin with the fork. Simply pick up the fork and put it in your open, flat palm. Hold it so it balances along your left index finger. Now, pick up the knife with your right hand and hold it so that the blade is facing upward and resting along your right index finger. Then, wrap all of the other fingers into the palm of your hand. Finally, flip your wrists around so that they are now facing the plate. You should have flat index fingers (no McDonald's arches!) and also make sure that your index fingers are on the handle of each piece of cutlery and not on the bridge, prongs, or blade of the fork and knife. And, voilà! That was easy, and you look fabulous. In the next chapter (page 123) I'll teach you how to cut and eat correctly with cutlery. If you are eating a dish that requires only one piece of cutlery such as a soup spoon or salad fork, then it's rather easy. Hold it in your dominant hand with the bowl of the spoon or prongs of the fork facing upward. Your index and thumb are on the top of the spoon and the other fingers are wrapped into your palm.

Step 1: Balance the back of the utensil along your index fingers

Step 2: Wrap your remaining fingers around the handle

Step 3: Twist your wrists so the blade of the knife and prongs of the fork are facing the plate

Step 4: When holding one piece of cutlery, use your dominant hand with fork prongs facing upward

Resting Cutlery

After a maximum of four bites, take a break. To signal to service staff that we are doing so, there is a position we take on. At the end of the meal there is also a position we rest our silverware in to show the server we are finished and that they can clear the plate. This is how we communicate with service staff without speaking to them constantly. In modern formal etiquette, we say "server," not "waiter" or "waitress."

Break position of cutlery

Finished position of cutlery

American vs Continental

If you are dining at an informal restaurant or home in America, it's perfectly fine to eat in the "American" style. That being said, as soon as you go to a formal dinner at a private home or restaurant, I recommend switching to the Continental style, which is seen as more formal.

American Style: Resting the knife on the plate and eating with the fork prongs up

Continental Style: Holding both the knife and fork at the same time

Modern Etiquette Made Easy

Identifying Cutlery

A: Main dining fork; B: Fish fork; C: Salad/Appetizer fork; D: Dessert fork; E: Oyster fork; F: Soup spoon for clear broth or stew; G: Soup spoon for cream broth/Stew; H: Serving spoon (can come in many sizes); I: Teaspoon/Dessert spoon; J: Demitasse spoon for espresso; K: Main dining knife; L: Appetizer knife; M: Fish knife; N: Butter knife

118

Meier Method of Table Setting

It's important to know how to set a table no matter if you do it regularly or not. In my courses I have all students set a table, even if they insist that they never will again. The reason is because if you can set a table by putting all the pieces where they belong, you won't forget where everything belongs when you sit at a table to dine. For a basic table setting in the Western world, the Meier Method of Table Setting is an easy way to remember which side of the table all the pieces go on.

Let's look at the fork. It typically has four prongs, and the word left has four letters.

F-O-R-K

L-E-F-T

So, you know that the fork goes on the left of the table setting.

The word knife has five letters, and the word right has five letters, so we know the knife goes on the right.

K-N-I-F-E

R-I-G-H-T

Now, the spoon has five letters and so does the word right, so we know the spoon goes on the right as well.

Service plates, often called chargers, are set in American dining for either decoration or to protect a table from heat or condensation. We never eat directly off of a service plate. You can use service plates in one of two ways: If you intend for it to be purely decorative, then they may be removed as soon as the guests are seated (often seen at fine dining restaurants). Alternatively, you can leave them down throughout the first course and then clear them before the main dining plate is placed on the table (more traditionally seen at private home dinner parties). The service plate is always cleared off of the table before the main course is served.

Table Setting Examples

In this section, I will show you a few examples of American table setting pending the number of courses you are having. Remember the table setting in Western countries can change depending on the country you are in. The British or French table settings, for example, look very different to that of the American. The key with table settings is to remember that you only set the table with the pieces your guest will need to enjoy the meal. Here are some examples for both informal and formal American table settings. The first example would be what you would see for a two-course meal with soup and a main course. The second example would be what you would see for a four-course meal with a soup, starter, main, and dessert. Easy, right? Now, let's talk about how to navigate a place setting with multiple courses.

Navigating Multiple Courses

Imagine you sit down to a meal at a restaurant which is going to be six courses. Where do you start? With the exception of France, in Western dining there should only ever be a maximum of eight pieces of silverware on the table at once, with the ninth piece being an oyster fork as an exception. If you have twelve courses, for example, the silverware should be reset with the course it is being served with rather than laying out more than the allotted silverware allowed to be set at a table. Remember that bread never counts as a course.

You've probably heard the general rule of thumb to start from the outside and work your way in. One thing I like to add to that is you typically start on the side that has the most pieces of cutlery. So,

Intro to Dining

Example of an informal two-course American meal (including soup, entrée, bread, water)

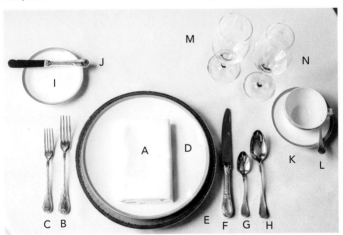

Example of an informal four-course American meal (including soup, salad or starter, entrée, dessert, bread, water, wine, coffee/tea)

A: Napkin; B: Main dining fork; C: Dining plate; D: Soup bowl; E: Main dining knife; F: Soup spoon; G: Bread plate; H: Butter knife; I: Salt and pepper; J: Place card; K: Water glass

A: Napkin; B: Main dining fork; C: Luncheon fork; D: Dining plate; E: Service plate (a.k.a charger); F: Main dining knife; G: Dessert spoon; H: Soup spoon; I: Bread plate; J: Butter knife; K: Coffee or tea cup; L: Teaspoon; M: Water glass; N: Wine glass

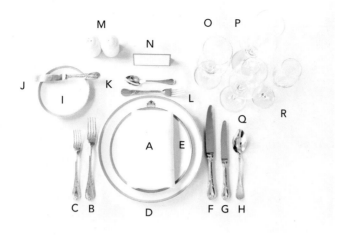

Example of a formal four-course American meal (including soup, starter, entrée, dessert, bread, water, red wine, white wine, champagne)

if there is a fork on the left and a knife and spoon on the right side of the plate, you know you should pick up the spoon first. Now if the table is set with equal numbers on both sides, say a main dining fork and knife and a starter fork and knife, then you know you should pick up each side together.

A: Napkin; B: Main dining fork; C: Luncheon fork; D: Main dining plate; E: Starter plate; F: Main dining knife; G: Luncheon knife; H: Soup spoon; I: Bread plate; J: Butter knife; K: Dessert spoon; L: Dessert fork; M: Salt and pepper; N: Place card; O: Water glass; P: White wine glass; Q: Red wine glass; R: Champagne flute

Chapter 9

Ooh Là Là!
Formal Dining

When you think of where you will use your formal dining skills, you might think of a very nice restaurant. Some people like to call fine dining or formal dining "fancy." I really don't like or use this word because I think if you describe a place or style as fancy it points out that you are not used to it, which there is no need to point out. Remember, you will only look like a fish out of water if you act like one. Instead, you might say you are going to a formal restaurant, or even an exceptional restaurant.

Formal Dining Tips

Each year at Beaumont Etiquette we teach etiquette to thousands of people around the globe. Often when it comes to dining we see the same questions asked and the same rules broken, so I thought it might be helpful to list the most common dining faux pas and how to prevent them.

1. **Always wait until everyone has their food before you begin.**
   If you are sitting at a table with more than ten seats, wait until everyone around you has their food and then begin. If your food is delayed coming to the table, it's up to you to say "please go ahead and enjoy while it's still warm."

2. **The host should always say "please enjoy," not bon appétit.** In France, this phrase translates to "good digestion" which to some people could be considered grotesque to talk about the physical digestion process. Instead, the French say the equivalent of "enjoy your lunch" which is what I recommend also saying in formal dining as a more elegant option.

3. **Take a maximum of four bites and then go into "break mode" by signaling with your silverware.** Eating too fast is simply seen as bad etiquette at the dining table. Only cut one piece of the food you are eating at a time. Only for small children do we chop up the whole chicken breast at once.

4. **Communal foods are never eaten directly from a shared plate.** Instead, take something off the communal plate and put it onto your own, then eat off of your plate or out of a cocktail napkin in your hand, depending on what you are eating. This could be a meal of tapas, hors d'oeuvres at a cocktail party, or even peanuts at a hotel bar.

5. **We pass everything around the table to the right with our right hand.** Our left hand is where you can sneeze or cough into if you need (then go wash!). Our right hands are open to shaking others and also to passing dishes. The exception would be if you were sitting around a table and either of the two people to your left asked for something, in which case you would hand it directly to them. Alternatively, you always pass to the right. If you need to lift your bum out of your seat to pass across the table, you should still pass to the right.

6. **Use your cutlery in the Continental style whenever you are in a formal social or business environment.**

7. **Handbags and briefcases:** The message you send by putting your handbag on the floor is that there is nothing of value in it. If your bag is large like a briefcase and you don't want to check it because

of its contents, it goes underneath the table by your top left toe so that it stays out of the way of service staff coming and going from the sides of the table. I advise thinking ahead before you choose a bag for a formal meal; try something small that can either fit behind your back or a very thin clutch that can go in your lap.

8. **Ring around the glass, a.k.a. "lip/lipstick rings":** When drinking out of a cup without a handle, it's hard to keep track of where your lips have touched the glass. If you have natural oils on your lips, Chapstick, grease from foods, or lipstick, you may have noticed when you look down at the glass what we call a "lip ring" or your lip mark smudged around the entire glass. Try to avoid this by consciously sipping from the same place on the glass each time. A lip ring around a glass often is distracting and can be unappetizing to look at over dinner or a cocktail party. Have a drink from a can or a bottle? Please immediately beeline over to the bar and ask for a glass to pour it in. We never saw Jackie O sipping out of a beer can, now did we?

9. **Seating:** If there is a table with a chair or bench, the VIP gets the bench seating, as it's typically more comfortable, gives a place to put things such as a handbag, and usually has the best view of the restaurant.

10. **Place cards:** When hosting at home, it's up to the host to decide where everyone sits. All of your guests should have place cards but you should not set them for yourself as the host. They can be placed at the top of the dessert cutlery or to the left of them.

11. **Grooming at the table:** Zero grooming at the table, please! All grooming should be done in private. This includes everything from using toothpicks to reapplying lipstick at the table. If you have long hair, it should be pushed back behind your shoulders before the meal begins.

12. **Cell phone etiquette:** Nothing should be on the table that is not a part of the meal, from cell phones to sunglasses. Cell phones should be left on vibrate, and no taking pictures of food at a formal dining table. If you are expecting an important call, simply tell the person you are dining with at the beginning of the meal that you are expecting that call, then put your phone on vibrate and under the side of your leg, screen facing up. When it vibrates and you see it's the important call you were waiting for, simply excuse yourself and leave the table. Do not take the call at the table and walk away from the dining area to do so.

13. **Salt and pepper:** Salt and pepper is always passed together in a pair.

14. **Seasoning your food:** Never season your food if the chef is within eyesight of the table, as you may offend them by doing so. Yes, even if they put salt and pepper on the table, trust me, a chef will notice when you season their food, which would imply they didn't do a good enough job themselves!

15. **Always match the number of courses the guest of honor is ordering.** It is very awkward if your date, for instance, only orders a salad and you order a soup, salad, and main course. Then, the date you presumably are trying to show respect to, is stuck waiting for you to finish. Dessert is the exception, as there is no pressure to order dessert, but if everyone else has dessert I would order a cup of tea or something to have in front of me.

16. **Most expensive items on a menu:** If you are a guest at a table, never order the most expensive item on a menu, from the meal to the wine. If you are paying, then go for it!

17. **Pace yourself:** Remember, when the Queen of England is finished at the dining table, that means everyone should be finishing right about the same time. She should never be stuck watching as others eat while she waits. So, how does this fit into

your modern life? The most VIP person at the table takes on the Queen/King role so that when they are finished, you want to pace yourself so that you finish at approximately the same time or within a couple of minutes after they put their cutlery down.

18. **No clinking in formal dining:** This rule does not apply to sitting at a casual pub or restaurant, but more for fine dining or at a private home where they have used delicate crystal. By raising a glass and "clinking" to say cheers or to toast, you may clink too hard and crack the glass. How mortifying would that be to have to tell the host! My fabulous mother-in-law is from Argentina and along with my Swiss father-in-law, this couple has the most discerning taste. As a wedding gift, they gave me and my husband the most stunning green vintage champagne flutes from Buenos Aires and my heart nearly broke when after a party I noticed half of them had cracks down the side. My husband makes me feel better, however, and says it's a sign of a good party. I will smile and leave it at that.

19. **Soup is the only food in Western dining that we eat by scooping away from us.** Never fill the bowl of the spoon all the way when scooping back. Never blow on your soup to cool it down as it could fly off the spoon onto the table. The correct way to stir soup to cool it off is by stirring in the shape of a half-moon crescent at the top of your soup plate. The only two countries in which it is seen as okay in formal etiquette to use bread to dunk or sop up soup or sauce are France and Italy.

20. **Never be rude to service staff:** This is my greatest dining pet peeve of them all. Everyone at some point in their social or professional lives has likely been embarrassed by how someone treats the service staff, and it is horrifically cringeworthy to witness. Remember to always treat service staff with the utmost respect, as that is someone's mother, father, brother, sister, or friend. I have

zero tolerance for rudeness toward people who are trying to help you. My team and I have had the great privilege to work in some of the most historic homes, palaces, and largest privately owned estates on earth. The families who inhabit them have one thing in common when it comes to their dining staff. They are incredibly polite and respectful. The Queen of England is even known to be quite close with many of her long-term service staff. People like the Queen are used to being served, and it's no big deal to have someone waiting on them hand and foot. Now, I find that people who are rude and disrespectful to service staff often did not grow up with this privilege and education of etiquette. I find these people often have an insecurity about wealth and ego and have to prove to everyone around them, including the service staff, that they are more powerful than them and will need to assert their dominance over them to make themselves feel more confident and secure. How to handle bad etiquette by another adult at the dining table? We ignore it, because pointing out bad etiquette *is* bad etiquette. For instance, if someone is eating something incorrectly, you could make someone feel bad about themselves by correcting them, which in turn is bad etiquette.

Afternoon Tea

Let's chat afternoon tea. Whether you are throwing your own tea party, attending an afternoon tea, or with me in class having tea at The Plaza Hotel, there are a few important rules that will help you look incredibly elegant and be ready for Buckingham Palace!

Holding a coffee cup is very different from holding a teacup in formal etiquette. When holding the coffee cup or mug, we loop our index finger through the cup handle and put our thumb on the top of the handle. For a teacup, it's a bit different. We typically have less tea served in a cup than coffee, and oftentimes the cups are made of more delicate material such as bone china. As the coffee cup is therefore heavier, we need more support through our index finger to hold it. We hold the teacup by pinching our index finger with our thumb and then lining our middle finger along the bottom of the handle to support it. Think "pinch and support." It may feel funny at first if you are not used to this method of holding, and if that is the case, you can use your index and middle finger

Holding a coffee cup

Holding a teacup

from your other hand to hold and support it from the other side.

Here are my top ten rules to follow to be perfectly polished while enjoying afternoon tea:

1. **It's called "afternoon tea," not "high tea."** (Although the Queen just calls it "tea.") Afternoon tea is served traditionally from 3 to 5 p.m. with tea, crustless sandwiches, scones, and desserts. High tea is more of a meal, served early evening around

Formal tea tier

5 p.m., and would likely consist of a meat dish with tea.

2. **The saucer stays on the table throughout afternoon tea and is not held while sitting at the table enjoying tea.** Only if you

stand or are sitting where no table is in front of you should you hold both your saucer and teacup together.

3. **How to hold a teacup properly . . . it will take practice!**

4. **The handle of the teacup stays at three o'clock, unless you are left-handed, then you turn it to nine o'clock.**

5. **Never create a "whirlpool" when stirring your tea (either clockwise or counterclockwise).** Instead, stir your tea from twelve o'clock to six o'clock.

6. **Don't add cream to your tea, only milk.** The hot liquid goes in first followed by the cold (milk).

7. **When pouring loose-leaf tea from a teapot, always use a strainer, which is placed over your teacup and then removed before drinking.** You would not be served tea bags at the palace for formal tea. Now, if you are using a tea bag for a single serving of tea, do not drink your cup of tea with the tea bag still floating inside. It causes a mess as it bobs around while you try to take sips. Instead, take it out by pulling the

Pouring tea

string with your left hand and gently pressing the excess water into the cup with the back of your spoon and squeezing the tea bag against the inside of your cup. Do not take the string and wind it around your spoon to try and squeeze out the water with your fingers.

8. **If someone is pouring tea for you and asks you to pass your teacup to them, pass with both the saucer and teacup.**

9. **The correct order to enjoy food at afternoon tea is savory to sweet—sandwiches first, then scones (pronounced scōne in the US and sk-on in the UK) and finally sweets.** You can use your fingers to eat all three courses. To eat a scone, simply break it in half with your fingers. Put the clotted cream on first, followed by the berry jam or lemon curd provided on top if you wish. Oh, and one last thing. When

Afternoon tea sweets

you are breaking open your scone, don't use a knife to cut it; it should be broken with your fingers. (The only bread we cut is when it is served on our plates as part of our meal, like brioche toast with scrambled eggs and salmon, for example.) Break off the one piece of the scone you plan to eat at a time and then put the clotted cream and/or jam on it, and enjoy! It is risky bringing an entire scone up to your mouth all deliciously buttered, as scones tend to be very flaky and may break apart on the way up to your mouth.

10. **Never put your pinkie out!** Never. Not for wine or water or even coffee and tea. If you do, you may wonder where this came from in the first place, and there is actually a historical reason for it. When the tea trade routes first opened in Europe in the 1600s, if you had tea you were one of the wealthiest people on the planet. You would just be served a small amount in a tiny, delicate cup without a handle, which was what the tea was served in from Asia. As the trade routes opened, tea became less

expensive and therefore more widely available and larger quantities could be enjoyed at once. Because there was no handle, when someone drank from the cup, often the pinkie finger naturally would come out for balance. However, once the Germans invented the handle to the cup in 1707, it allowed for larger quantities of tea to be held in one cup. And with the birth of the handle, the pinkie finger was no longer needed, and it went in . . . never to return again!

Cocktail Party Etiquette Tips

- Always take the cocktail napkin first, followed by the hors d'oeuvres.

- Only take one hors d'oeuvre at a time.

- Never take anything directly off of the server's plate and put it into your mouth. When food is communal, it's always taken off the plate and transferred onto your plate or napkin and then eaten off of that.

- Only take hors d'oeuvres that are bite sized. The point of a cocktail party is to mingle and be able to speak without large mouthfuls of food. If you are planning a cocktail party, choose your hors d'oeuvre menu wisely. Always think about serving foods that will not cause the fingers to be too greasy in addition to being too large. No lamb shanks on a plate, please.

- Choose one, either an hors d'oeuvre *or* a drink. Try not to walk around with both hands full.

- Where possible hold your glass of wine or your drink in your left hand so that your right hand is free to shake or greet people.

If you have a plate of food, a cocktail napkin, and a glass, you can briefly balance the stem of the glass on your plate by holding it all with your left hand, then returning the glass to your right hand when you're able. You can also use this trick with a clutch handbag.

Meier Method Step 5

PRACTICE

Congratulations! You have made it through the first four steps of the Meier Method. Next, in step five, it's time to continue putting what you learned into practice every day. Now you are really ready to start socializing and getting out of your comfort zone. Once you are out and about, you'll need to be prepared to receive and send out invitations, attend different social gatherings, and send handwritten thank-you letters. The most common group gatherings are weddings and baby showers and of course your general dinner party, so we'll cover the top etiquette conundrums of those three so that you can be a superstar at every occasion.

Chapter 10

Special Occasion Social Etiquette

Stationery

Everyone should have their own stationery and use it. Because so few people use it nowadays and default to email for communication, when people do send handwritten notes, it truly stands out and gives added impact. It doesn't need to be custom, but if you have your monogram or name printed on the cards at the top center or bottom right-hand corner, it is always an impressive touch. Stationery can be used to send a note to say hello or as a tangible form of gratitude. Are handwritten notes outdated? That question hurts my heart, but I hear it all the time. The answer is no! I strongly believe that a handwritten thank-you letter is still so important because it shows added impact. In a time when people are so used to communicating electronically, it's so lovely and always a surprise to receive a handwritten thank-you note. It means the person took the time to show thanks, making the recipient feel special. Now, do I think you always have to send a handwritten thank-you note? No. With modern etiquette, I believe and teach that you should match the formality of the thank-you with the way you thank someone. For instance, if your neighbor leaves a little candy cane in your mailbox for the holidays, a nice thank-you email is perfectly appropriate. If someone invites you over for a formal dinner party at their home, a formal thank-you letter in the form of a handwritten thank-you note would be more appropriate. If you get married, hand-written thank-you notes are a must in my book and they should go out within three months of the wedding day or when you receive the gift after the wedding day. If you ever want to add emphasis to show thanks, when in doubt, go with handwritten stationery.

Writing Thank-You Notes

Try not to start a thank-you note with "thank you." Yes, you read that correctly! Even the Kennedys followed this rule when sending out the thousands of thank-you letters they had to write while in office at The White House. The reason is because a letter loses impact when it starts with the expected. You should still include the words "thank you" in your letter, just not as the first line. Instead, follow my formula to a great thank-you letter:

Dear XX,

How something made you feel: i.e. I was so excited when I opened . . .

Why you love(d) it: i.e. A XX has been on my wish list for ages and I have been using it every day.

"Thank you for . . .": i.e. Thank you for such a thoughtful gift.

Closing: i.e. I'm so looking forward to seeing you next month.

Best Wishes,
XX

You can also sign off with Sincerely, Love, or whatever sign-off to mirror your relationship with the person. Just remember we reserve the word "sincerely" for letter writing and "best regards/warmest regards/with regards or best wishes" for formal emails.

Picking out Stationery

Whether you buy it at a mass retailer online or have your own made, you may want to keep the following components in mind when picking out stationery:

Card stock: Refers to the thickness of the paper. It's important not to choose card stock that is too flimsy or thin, and the thickness of the stock can range anywhere from 45# to 200#. In America you may see it listed as # or lbs. For a nice thick stationery, I recommend choosing a thickness that is 96# or higher. Cotton is a lovely choice of material for card stock.

Sizing: For correspondence cards, sizing may vary, but typical sizing is 4.5 x 6, give or take a little, as each brand typically has their own exact stylistic measurements. For a classic and elegant choice, I like flat stationery cards for my formal correspondence cards with a monogram engraved on it. If you prefer a folded correspondence card, that's perfectly fine as well, as it's purely a matter of style.

Addressing Letters and Envelopes

When you address an envelope of a card or invitation, here is my quick guide to whose name comes first in modern etiquette. If you don't know the gender of the person you are addressing, such as with the gender-neutral name Jamie Boe, do not use any title.

Addressing a letter to a woman:

We use "Miss" when addressing a woman under the age of eighteen years old. Once she reaches adulthood, you switch to Ms. If you are addressing a woman and you don't know if she is married or not, it's best to stick to Ms.

- The woman is married and decides to use her husband's name socially:
  - Ex: Mrs. David Lander
  - Ex: Mrs. Jessica Lander
- The woman is married and decides to keep her maiden name:
  - Ex: Ms. Jessica Lander
- The woman is separated but not divorced:
  - Ex: Mrs. David Lander
  - Ex: Mrs. Jessica Lander
  - Ex: Ms. Jessica Lander
- The woman is divorced:
  - Ex: Ms. Jessica Lander
  - Ex: Ms. Jessica Pozzi (her maiden name)

Addressing a letter to a couple:

Traditionally, a woman's name followed a man's name on an envelope address so that his first name and surname were not separated (David and Jessica Lander). In modern etiquette, which name comes first does not matter and to write it either way is perfectly appropriate. I personally prefer to use the second address Mr. and Mrs. Meier, as I feel it's more modern than only listing the man's name.

- Unmarried couple living together:
  - Ex: Mr. David Lander and Ms. Jessica Pozzi
- A married couple where the wife uses her husband's name socially:
  - Ex: Mr. and Mrs. David Lander
  - Ex: Mr. and Mrs. Lander
- Couple with children:
  - The best way to do this is, is to write the family's first name(s) followed by the last.

- Married couple with children:
  - Ex: The Lander Family
- Unmarried couple with children:
  - Ex: The Lander-Pozzi Family
- Married couple (male & female):
  - Ex: Mr. David Lander and Mrs. Jessica Lander
  - Ex: Mrs. Jessica Lander and Mr. David Lander
- Married couple (the wife uses her maiden name):
  - Ex: Mr. David Lander and Mrs. Jessica Pozzi
  - Ex: Mrs. Jessica Pozzi and Mr. David Lander
- Married couple (same gender couple with same marital last name):
  - Ex: Mr. Gordon and Mr. Robert Smith
- Married couple (same gender couple with different last name):
  - Ex: Mrs. Mey Walter and Mrs. Aruna Carter
- A woman whose title outranks her husband's:
  - Dr. Amy Mero and Mr. Lyndon Mero

Note: If ever one half of the couple "outranks" the other, which is usually seen through a title (such as Dr.), the name of the person who possesses the higher rank comes first. In modern etiquette, the gender no longer matters, and it's simply to show respect that the highest-ranking person be listed first.

- Widowed:
  - Ex: Mrs. Joseph Smith
  - Ex: Mrs. Natalie Smith (still include her married last name)

Note: While both examples are appropriate, I personally would recommend going with Mrs. Natalie Smith, as she may feel an emotional chord of sadness when seeing his name following her loss. That being said, the former style of using his name for a widow is considered traditional.

Signing Cards or Correspondence

When signing off a holiday card for instance, the traditional way is with a salutation followed by the parents' names then children listed from eldest to youngest. Traditionally it was the male's name first followed by the female's and children's names, but now with same sex marriages and families, as long as you have the adult names first followed by children in order of age, it's just perfect!

RSVP Etiquette

If you are sending out an invitation, there is no need to write "Please RSVP" because the RSVP part is an acronym for répondez s'il vous plaît, meaning "please respond" in French. By adding a please in front of the RSVP, you are being redundant.

How to fill out a RSVP card:

If you get invited to a more formal event such as a wedding you may receive an RSVP card with the invitation. You should simply write your name(s) on the line and then check any relevant boxes. The M is to fill in the blank as in Mr., Mrs., Ms., or Miss. I will never forget being invited to my aunt's wedding as a teenager and receiving an RSVP card and writing Myka on the line, thinking the M was for my first initial. Still makes me smile and cringe at the same time.

How to Be a Great Host

The main goal of a host is to instantly make your guests feel welcome, comfortable, and happy. All three of those things are very different, but equally important. When I host people at my home, I like to have festive music playing to set the mood for the evening, have a tray of beautiful drinks to offer straightaway, the smell of something fabulous cooking, and the biggest smile on my face when my guests arrive.

Don't be afraid to delegate duties. I put my husband on jacket and drink duty (always make sure drinks are flowing upon arrival). Even getting your children to be the table setters or greeters is a wonderful way to incorporate them. If you set the table ahead of time, don't put any food or drinks (not even water!) on the table ahead of your guests arriving. A little flyaway piece of fuzz landing in your guests' water is not a great way to start a dinner party. All food and beverages should be served upon your guests sitting. Remember, a beautifully set table shows your guests you took the time to prepare and create a special experience for them.

One of the most important things is to organize and plan ahead. Think of everything a guest will need before they even know it. With every dinner or cocktail party, I work backward to make a list and timeline of what I need and when. Pending the event, your list may include food, drinks, grocery shopping, buying decorations, setting the table, cooking, cleaning, sending invitations, having RSVPs by date, or sending reminders forty-eight hours before the event. Remember to always prepare more than enough food and drinks and have enough prepared and cooked before your guests arrive so you can enjoy their company and host them without feeling bogged down with tasks.

If it's a formal dinner party that I am hosting and someone asks to bring something, my answer is always the same: "Please just bring your appetite!" I think if you are hosting a formal party, it's your responsibility to take care of your guests and not put the stress on them to bring things. If it's a casual gathering of old friends, a potluck may be your thing and that's perfectly fine, but the moment we go formal I recommend preparing everything so people can just show up and enjoy. I feel the same about clearing and cleaning. If guests offer to help clean, my answer is always "Thank you, you're too kind, but I have a system and it's a bit faster if I just take care of it myself. Please sit and relax and I'll just be a moment." In fact, I am rather insistent that my guests don't help clean. As a great host, I want everyone to come over, enjoy, and not lift a finger so that they feel truly spoiled. I never clean while a guest is in my home, and always put things aside to do once they leave.

Dietary Restrictions

As soon as people RSVP, make sure to ask if there are any dietary restrictions or allergies and be sure to accommodate them all. If you forget to ask and you end up serving shellfish for dinner and your guest announces when they see the scallops hit the table that they are allergic, your dinner party just went from fabulous to flop and it could have been easily avoided. I always make sure that for every three guests, I have at least two food options for cocktail parties, with one of those always being vegetarian. For instance, if you have six guests, I will have at least four hors d'oeuvres on offer, with at least two of those options vegetarian. Once you hit nine guests or more, this rule no longer applies.

Cheese Boards

An easy food option for a cocktail party is a cheese board. To slice cheese, (note that we never say "cut" cheese!) you want to always slice along the long side of the cheese. Why not off the bottom of the cheese, farthest away from the rind? The rind is considered the most tasteless part of the cheese, and by slicing off at the other end of the rind, you are taking the tastiest part and leaving the cheese slices closest to the tasteless rind for everyone else. See? There is even good cheese etiquette.

Always start by serving left to right a hard, then soft, then bleu cheese in that order because we often pick left to right, so we want the most flavorful cheeses last so it doesn't obstruct the taste of the more delicate flavors. Make sure to always have at least three options on every cheese board so you can accommodate every tasting palate. Depending on the pairing of the wine I have, I like to serve dried meats, nuts like almonds, dried fruits like apricot, and olives. Remember that the cheese is the masterpiece and the crackers should not be flavored strongly. I recommend water crackers which are lightly flavored so the cheese remains the star.

The one thing never to put on your cheese board if you are serving it with wine? Grapes! I know what you may be thinking . . . that you have been serving cheese with grapes and wine your whole life. The reason we don't serve grapes with wine is because they can clash with one another. Wine is made from grapes, as we know, and fresh fruit tends to have high acidity and can be tart, distorting the taste of the wine. Grapes especially may clash because there is already a specific blend or one type of grape in the wine, and anything else may ruin the flavor if paired together.

Wine Temperatures When Serving

It's important to serve wine at the correct temperature as varied temperatures can change the taste and smell of wine.

40–50°F: Champagne and sparkling wine

Note that it is only officially "champagne" if it comes from the Champagne region in France. Therefore, there is no such thing as California Champagne . . . it would be considered sparkling wine from California. You can pop a bottle in an ice bucket for about thirty to forty minutes and that tends to do the trick.

50–60°F: White, rosé, and light reds

There is nothing worse in wine-speak than taking a sip on a hot day of your warm white wine! Avoid ice in wine always; it waters it down and is seen as a wine sin.

60–65°F: Full-bodied reds

There is a common misperception that all reds are served at room temperature. This is quite incorrect. Depending on the red wine, the preferred serving temperature can vary substantially.

Tips to Be a Great Dinner Party Host

- Lay out your place setting and table decor at least one day in advance. You can have the table beautifully decorated and set ahead to help you focus on preparing the food.

- Ensure your table decor (including flowers and tall candles) does not block the view across the table.

- Prepare as many dishes as you possibly can ahead of your guest arrivals so that you can be ready to entertain instead of rushing around in the kitchen. I suggest having some light hors d'oeuvres and drinks to serve when guests arrive, as they'll come hungry and it may take time to get all the food on the table.

- Serve children and the elderly their food first, followed by the most VIP female followed by all the other females (after the most VIP female, serve the other females in the order they are sitting at the table), then the most VIP male followed by all of the other males. The host(s) will serve themselves last.

🎀 Traditionally, the most VIP person sits to the right of the host. If possible for mixed gender dinner parties, try to seat man-woman-man-woman. Also, don't seat couples next to one another unless they are celebrating a special occasion, such as an engagement, birthday, even a housewarming. You can sit them near one another, or even catty-corner.

🎀 Turn off TV during the meal and put on seasonal music instead. This will help everyone enjoy both the food and the company all the more!

🎀 Be overprepared: plan for plenty of food and drinks if possible so that if someone wants a second helping you can graciously serve.

🎀 Make sure to speak to and engage all of your guests. A gracious host or hostess will make sure everyone at the table is happy, comfortable, and feels welcome. If guests do not know one another, be sure to introduce before they are all seated.

🎀 If you say prayers in your home before meals, never feel the need to stop if the guest does not share your faith. As they are a guest in your home, they should follow the customs and culture of your family. They do not need to participate if they do not wish.

🎀 There is no need to say "ladies first" anymore when serving food or allowing a lady to walk through a doorway or take something from the meal first. In modern etiquette we no longer need to verbally point out gender, and instead should simply say, "Please, after you."

🎀 At a restaurant, if you are the host, you pay. This is not only hosting, but also dating etiquette 101. It no longer has to do with gender but instead who invited the other person. If you invite the person out on a date, choose the restaurant, order the wine, and play host, then you also pay. That being said, I think it's always excellent etiquette to offer to pay if you are a guest.

- Cocktail parties are the hardest because people lose track of time when they have been drinking. For a really late night that seems to never end, my trick (while a more modern and certainly not formal etiquette!) after a great cocktail party to get people home is tequila. Yes, that's what I said. If it's way past the time I thought people would be staying until, I pull out the old hard liquor bar cart and let them at it. Within the next 30 minutes, I'm usually calling cabs for everyone per their request.

Guest Etiquette

Tips to Be a Great Dinner Party Guest

The number one rule to remember is never show up empty-handed. I mean literally never. Remember to never show up early, and when you do show up, make sure you're dressed to mirror the effort the host put into having you.

What to bring

When I RSVP to an invitation to a dinner party, I always ask what I can bring. Maybe the host assigns you something, at which point it's easy. If they don't, however, you should still bring a host(ess) gift. One of the golden rules of etiquette is to never show up emp-ty-handed. So, what are some things that you can bring? Try a lightly scented candle, a beautifully packaged box of home baked goods, macaroons, or chocolates. The best gifts are ones that have a good story behind them. I once had a friend arrive from Connecticut and she brought a jar of fresh honey from a farm stand near her home along with a wooden honey scoop, which was such a great gift as it had a story and was a treat! If you know the host really well, bring something you know they would love. If Kari loves hosting cocktail parties, I might bring her some fun, embroidered cocktail napkins for instance.

What are two things *not* to bring to a formal dinner party? Many of you reading this may be shocked to read what they are:

1. **Wine:** Unless the person specifically asks you to bring wine, I always say it's just not the best thing to show up with. Imagine if I am preparing a dinner of angel hair pasta with a white fish and white wine sauce with asparagus and you show up with your bottle of red Malbec. I, as the host, feel pressure to now serve your bottle, which may clash with what I'm preparing. That being said, if you are at the receiving end of a host(ess) gift, you should never feel obligated to open a gift. You can put it away for a rainy day, or keep it out if you'd like. It's your call. The other reason I don't think wine is the best option is because it implies the person you are visiting didn't have the caliber of wine you wished for. This could offend the host.

2. **Flowers:** Not only do flowers all have meaning, but your host could be highly allergic. The main reason, however, is imagine that I invite six guests over for cocktails and snacks. Kelli arrives to my home first and hands me a bouquet of flowers. It's correct etiquette to display them and I therefore have to go to the kitchen, find a vase, and fill it with water and arrange them to put out. Meanwhile, when I was tending to my hostess gift, I missed my chance to welcome Lisa, who just arrived a couple of moments after Kelli. Therefore, you always want to bring a gift that doesn't create more work for the host. If you love sending flowers and you know the host enjoys them, you have a few options. You can

bring an arrangement that is already in a vase, or send an arrangement ahead of time. On Thanksgiving, for instance, my mother sends a festive cornucopia to the host the morning of the dinner.

Housekeeping Rules

Make sure to offer to take off your shoes if you see the host welcome you without shoes on or there are obvious signs at the door where shoes are lined up. If you are staying at a home overnight, make sure to leave nothing behind, meaning clean up after yourself. I always ask my host what they would prefer me to do with any bedding or towels and follow instructions. If they say to just leave everything, I still always make the bed and put the towels up to hang nicely while drying.

Guest Dinner Party Etiquette

- If you have strict dietary requirements, make sure to notify your host or hostess when you RSVP. If you accept a dinner party invitation and your host does not ask for your dietary restrictions, it's important to let them know in plenty of time that you are not allowed to eat XYZ. The etiquette if you are allergic to shellfish, for example, is to tell your host but also at the same time offer a solution. "I would love to attend the dinner party, thank you for the invitation. I did want to let you know that I am allergic to shellfish, but if you planned to make a dish that had shellfish in it, I would be happy to bring a dish that doesn't have it that I can share with everyone." A good host will not allow you to do that and will accommodate your needs. Note it is impolite to tell someone your likes and dislikes; only report what you are unable to eat for dietary or allergy purposes.

- The perfect time to arrive to a private home is about ten minutes after the event start time. Never arrive early. Not even one minute early! This is important because the host or hostess is probably preparing last minute touches and will be caught off guard. When you arrive, offer to help in any way you can if you see they are still setting up.

- Always ask where the host would like you to sit before taking a seat at their table.

- Dress to impress: It's likely your host or hostess has spent hours if not days preparing. Mirror their effort and show respect, gratefulness, and enthusiasm for the day by dressing in the spirit of the evening.

- Always compliment a host on the meal they have served.

- After the host or hostess has given a toast, it is a lovely idea to give a thank-you toast, complimenting the chef and thanking him or her for the amazing day. When you toast, be sure to stand and raise your glass to the table when your toast is over. This signifies you are done and is a celebratory gesture to drink in the honor of the hostess.

- Always offer to help clean up. If you are at a dinner party, it's always a nice gesture. That being said, if a host says not to help, you should respect their wishes.

- Don't overstay your welcome: Plan to stay only thirty minutes after dessert and coffee. The host or hostess will be exhausted from cooking and entertaining and probably has quite a bit of cleaning and organizing to do post-meal.

- Thank-you letters are key. Within two days of the day, a handwritten thank-you letter in the mail is a gorgeous way of thanking your host for the lovely day.

- Have fun, be grateful, and always show respect to your host.

151

A Final Note

Phew! You made it! You should feel so proud and accomplished because you just got through the last chapter of the Five-Step Meier Method of Etiquette! Now, I know this is a lot to remember, but the most important part is to put everything you learned into practice. Remember, if you only use what you learned in this book for special occasions, it won't ever feel natural and you may even forget it. My goal of this book was to have you finish reading it feeling more confident than when you started. I truly hope you come out feeling strong, excited, and inspired to practice what you learned.

The key to master the last step of the Meier Method is to *practice!* Practice all the time. Try your new voice, new look, or new energy out on someone you pass by at the gas station or at the restaurant you go out to tonight. Practice out of context and whenever you can so it feels like everyday modern etiquette that is practical and easy to use.

The most important part of this book? If you took away nothing else, and I mean absolutely nothing, the most important thing is to remember to always be kind, respectful, and considerate to everything, everyone, and all living things around you. That, at the end of the day, is what etiquette is truly all about. Now, go out there and spread kindness like confetti, uplift others, spread joy, feel great, make others feel great, and make it count!

About the Author

If you can be nothing else, be kind
—Myka Meier

Named "America's Queen of Good Manners" by *The Times* magazine, Myka Meier proudly opened Beaumont Etiquette in 2013 to bring a fresh perspective to modern manners. Breaking down the stereotype that etiquette is outdated, inaccessible, or even a lost art form, she designed etiquette courses with a modern spin—that are not intimidating to learn. Myka's core belief is that etiquette is about being kind, respectful, and considerate to everyone and all living things around you.

After receiving a degree in communications in the United States, Myka moved to London where she had two years' experience working on a global endeavor initiated by its patron, His Royal Highness The Prince of Wales. She went on to study at multiple traditional etiquette programs in the United Kingdom, attended Swiss finishing school, and trained in London under a former member of The Royal Household Staff of Her Majesty the Queen.

In 2016 Myka co-founded The Plaza Hotel Finishing Program with Beaumont Etiquette. The program, which quickly became world-renowned for training adults, teens, and children in modern manners, continuously sells out year after year and has been cited as one of the nation's "Most Innovative Companies." In 2018, Beaumont Etiquette became the official etiquette partner of *Downton Abbey: The Exhibition*. Myka has been featured across global media including *The Today Show, The New York Times*, *Good Morning America*, and *People*, *TIME*, and *Vogue* magazines. Along with her team of instructors, Myka travels the country as a keynote speaker, training private social groups to Fortune 100 companies. An avid volunteer, Myka resides in New York with her Swiss husband and daughter. Find her website at beaumontetiquette.com and chat with her on Instagram, Twitter, or Facebook @mykameier.

Acknowledgments

Thank you to my amazing family, for without you, I'd be lost. Your unconditional love and positivity have shaped me into who I am today.

To my husband who supported me to go after my dream and encourages me daily. Oh, and thank you for suggesting I take an etiquette course ;)

A very special thank you to the beautiful Plaza Hotel and its wonderful team who welcomed me with open arms. I am beyond grateful for your partnership and continued support.

To the great Suzanne Lane, who believed in me from day one. Thank you for your mentorship and friendship.

With gratitude to Alexandra Messervy for your tutelage, support, mentorship, and for embracing my passion for etiquette.

Index

Index

Index